WORLD HISTORY

THE

INFORMATION REVOLUTION

Transforming the world through technology

By Tamra B. Orr

Portions of this book originally appeared in *The Information Revolution* by Stuart A. Kallen.

LUCENT PRESS

Published in 2020 by
Lucent Press, an Imprint of Greenhaven Publishing, LLC
353 3rd Avenue
Suite 255
New York, NY 10010

Designer: Deanna Paternostro
Editor: Diane Bailey

Cataloging-in-Publication Data

Names: Orr, Tamra B.
Title: The information revolution: transforming the world through technology / Tamra B. Orr.
Description: New York : Lucent Press, 2020. | Series: World history | Includes index.
Identifiers: ISBN 9781534567856 (pbk.) | ISBN 9781534567153 (library bound) | ISBN 9781534567863 (ebook)
Subjects: LCSH: Information technology–Juvenile literature. | Computer science–Juvenile literature.
Classification: LCC T58.5 O76 2020 | DDC 004–dc23

Printed in the United States of America

CPSIA compliance information: Batch #BS19KL: For further information contact Greenhaven Publishing LLC, New York, New York at 1-844-317-7404.

Please visit our website, www.greenhavenpublishing.com. For a free color catalog of all our high-quality books, call toll free 1-844-317-7404 or fax 1-844-317-7405.

Contents

Foreword

History books are often filled with names and dates—words and numbers for students to memorize for a test and forget once they move on to another class. However, what history books should be filled with are great stories, because the history of our world is filled with great stories. Love, death, violence, heroism, and betrayal are not just themes found in novels and movie scripts. They are often the driving forces behind major historical events.

When told in a compelling way, fact is often far more interesting—and sometimes far more unbelievable—than fiction. World history is filled with more drama than the best television shows, and all of it really happened. As readers discover the incredible truth behind the triumphs and tragedies that have impacted the world since ancient times, they also come to understand that everything is connected. Historical events do not exist in a vacuum. The stories that shaped world history continue to shape the present and will undoubtedly shape the future.

The titles in this series aim to provide readers with a comprehensive understanding of pivotal events in world history. They are written with a focus on providing readers with multiple perspectives to help them develop an appreciation for the complexity of the study of history. There is no set lens through which history must be viewed, and these titles encourage readers to analyze different viewpoints to understand why a historical figure acted the way they did or why a contemporary scholar wrote what they did about a historical event. In this way, readers are able to sharpen their critical-thinking skills and apply those skills in their history classes. Readers are aided in this pursuit by formally documented quotations and annotated bibliographies, which encourage further research and debate.

Many of these quotations come from carefully selected primary sources, including diaries, public records, and contemporary research and writings. These valuable primary sources help readers hear the voices of those who directly experienced historical events, as well as the voices of biographers and historians who provide a unique perspective on familiar topics. Their voices all help history come alive in a vibrant way.

As students read the titles in this series, they are provided with clear context in the form of maps, timelines, and informative text. These elements give them the basic facts they need to fully appreciate the high drama that is history.

The study of history is difficult at times—not because of all the information that needs to be memorized, but because of the challenging questions it asks us. How could something as horrible as the Holocaust happen? What are the roots of the struggle for peace in the Middle East? Why are some people reluctant to call themselves feminists? The information presented in each title gives readers the tools they need to confront these questions and participate in the debates they inspire.

As we pore over the stories of events and eras that changed the world, we come to understand a simple truth: No one can escape being a part of history. We are not bystanders; we are active participants in the stories that are being created now and will be written about in history books decades and even centuries from now. The titles in this series help readers gain a deeper appreciation for history and a stronger understanding of the connection between the stories of the past and the stories they are part of right now.

SETTING THE SCENE: A TIMELINE

1945 ·········· 1951 ·········· 1962 ·········· 1969 ·········· 1972 ·········· 1975 ·········· 1976 ··········

The first digital computer, the Electronic Numerical Integrator and Computer (ENIAC), is built at the University of Pennsylvania.

Leonard Kleinrock writes the first paper on packet switching, a concept that forms the basis of the internet.

Email is invented by engineer Ray Tomlinson.

The Advanced Research Projects Agency Network (ARPANET) is used for the first time.

Steven Jobs and Stephen Wozniak found Apple Computer.

The first mass-produced computer, the Universal Automatic Computer (UNIVAC), is delivered to the United States Census Bureau.

Paul Allen and Bill Gates found Microsoft.

1982 .... **1991** .... **1998** .... **2004** .... **2008** .... **2017** **2018**

TIME magazine selects the PC as "Machine of the Year."

Facebook is launched in Cambridge, Massachusetts.

Experts determine that Russian hackers attempted to influence the 2016 U.S. presidential election.

British scientist Tim Berners-Lee makes the web a publicly available service on the internet.

The Google searchable index catalogs 1 trillion unique URLs, or web addresses.

Larry Page and Sergey Brin launch Google Inc. in Menlo Park, California.

Net neutrality is repealed after being instituted in 2015.

THE END OF "I DON'T KNOW"

Throughout much of history, when a person was asked a question, it was perfectly acceptable to answer, "I don't know."

"Who wrote that?" "Hmmm, I don't know."
"What is today's forecast?" "I have no idea."
"When did that happen?" "Not a clue."

For all but the simplest questions, getting answers required going to the library, checking the TV or a newspaper, or asking an expert. If that was not possible, people just had to shrug their shoulders, say "I don't know," and move on. Now, almost everyone has the answers right at the ends of their fingertips or with the sound of their voice. Just ask a smartphone, type a few words on the computer, or consult your digital home assistant. The days of responding

with "I don't know" are gone, but this broad and simple access to information was unheard of even a generation ago.

One of the earliest milestones in what is often called the information revolution arrived in the 1400s when the printing press was invented. The world was transformed by the mass production of books. For the first time, people of most social and economic classes could own books, which allowed them to store and share information. Greater access to knowledge spurred innovation over the centuries, from the Renaissance that followed the Middle Ages to the Age of Enlightenment in the 18th century and the Industrial Revolution in the 19th century. Throughout this time, books were used to spark discussions about the human condition, explain historical events, delve into complex scientific and mathematical concepts, and put forth ideas for the future.

For five centuries, until the late 1900s,

The printing press had a tremendous impact on how people distributed and accessed information, leading to numerous advances in knowledge.

books and other printed materials were the main way to record and store human knowledge. Libraries grew and expanded, offering more people the opportunity to learn, discover, and read. They became the place where, as Italian author and philosopher Umberto Eco stated in 2007, the "collective wisdom" of people could be protected. "They were and still are a sort of universal brain where we can retrieve what we have forgotten and what we still do not know."[1]

As important and essential as libraries are, however, there is a growing number of people today who believe that printed books are on their way to becoming obsolete. Why bother to search dusty bookshelves for information when that same information is electronically available in seconds? Why buy a printed book when you can own it on your e-reader without leaving the house? Indeed, today's "universal brain" may live not so much in pages of print but instead in trillions of electrons pulsing through computers, the internet, and other electronic devices.

A Revolution of Knowledge

The transition from printed information to digital information began in the 1940s with the advent of the first computers and was catapulted forward with the development of the transistor and integrated circuit—or microchip—in the 1950s. Over the decades that have followed, these two inventions have drastically changed the way that people live and learn. Digital electronic devices and the internet have made the entire planet's collective

Compared to today's small laptops or tablets, computers of the past were huge. This early computer required an entire room.

history and knowledge available to the 4.2 billion people who visited cyberspace in 2018.

It is difficult to envision where computing eventually will take humankind. Changes are happening so rapidly that even experts struggle to predict what will happen next. There is no doubt, however, that the information revolution will keep impacting people's lives in expanding, and perhaps unexpected, ways.

CHAPTER ONE

A CALCULATED APPROACH

One glance around a school parking lot, a crowded train, or a waiting room makes it clear that many people use smartphones and other electronic devices to constantly stay informed, entertained, and connected. Many of us are so accustomed to these devices that it seems incredible that such small, powerful computers have been around for a relatively short time.

Atanasoff and Binary Numbers

For thousands of years, humans have developed mathematical concepts alongside spoken and written languages. People used numbers to chart the movement of the stars and planets, navigate across land and water, and measure dimensions to build structures. Numbers are also the basis for monetary systems and marking time. For generations, mathematical calculations were done in people's heads, with a pencil and paper, or by using only the simplest of tools, such as an abacus.

A machine could make the process of mathematical calculations much faster, and the purpose of the earliest computers came from the need to calculate and process numbers. One of the first electronic computers was developed by mathematician and inventor John Vincent Atanasoff, who had become intrigued as a child with number systems that used different bases.

Today, people primarily use a base 10 number system. Like it sounds, this system has 10 different numerals—1 through 9 and 0. Throughout history, however, people have used different systems. The ancient Babylonians, for instance, used base 60. Their influence is still felt today when telling time. Atanasoff was most interested in base 2, or the binary number system. Base 2 uses only 0s and 1s to represent all numbers. For example, the numbers 1, 2, 3, 4, and 5 would be written as 1, 10, 11, 100, and 101. Atanasoff could find no practical application for this particular system, but he was still fascinated by numbers, their patterns, and their potential uses.

Atanasoff decided to become a mathematician, and in 1930, after earning a master's degree in math and a doctorate in physics, he became an assistant professor of mathematics at Iowa State College (now called Iowa State University) in Ames, Iowa. However, he felt his work was limited by the lack of any machine that could help solve long, complex math problems more quickly and accurately than humans. During this era, calculators had giant metal wheels stamped with numbers. To perform calculations, these wheels were turned by hand using large cranks. Atanasoff was the first to call such machines "analog," because they used mechanical rather than electronic means to solve problems.

From ABC to ENIAC

Analog calculators were slow, prone to error, and unable to solve complex mathematical problems. Atanasoff wanted to build an electronic device to replace them. He imagined a machine that could calculate large numbers of equations simultaneously and quickly provide an accurate answer. He thought about such a machine for years but had little success coming up with a way that it would work.

Even calculators that were considered portable, such as this one from the 1940s, were large, heavy machines.

However, the story goes that one night in 1937, after having several drinks in a bar, the answers came to him, and Atanasoff solved the problem on a table napkin. As Jane Smiley wrote in her book, *The Man Who Invented the Computer: The Biography of John Atanasoff, Digital Pioneer*, "Whether he actually wrote about them on a napkin, nobody knows. But they came to him so forcefully that he maybe didn't need to write about them on a napkin. He just went home, found himself a graduate student and put it together."[2]

The machine used the binary number system Atanasoff favored and relied on electronic components, called capacitors, to represent the numbers. Capacitors with a positive charge would represent "1," and those with a negative charge would represent "0." To prevent them from losing their assigned values, the machine would periodically pass electricity through them in a technique called "jogging," which is still used today in computer memory chips. Atanasoff spent two years working with a student assistant, Clifford E. Berry, to build a calculating device. By October 1939, the men had constructed a prototype and called it the Atanasoff-Berry Computer, or ABC.

Over the next several years, Atanasoff and Berry perfected their invention. The final ABC was the size of a refrigerator, weighed more than 650 pounds (295 kg), and took 15 seconds to perform a calculation. It used 300 vacuum tubes, a type of capacitor used to control electrical signals.

With its tubes and wires, the ABC was extremely primitive by modern standards. Its vacuum tubes produced an enormous amount of heat, which was a downside. By using binary numbers and electronic elements to read and store data, however, the computer introduced important elements used in later machines.

In 1941, Atanasoff invited his friend, physicist John W. Mauchly, to Iowa to read his research papers and examine the ABC. Mauchly took many notes during his five-day visit and soon began work on his own computer. Later that year, in December 1941, the United States entered World War II, and the country's priorities changed. Work stopped on the ABC. Atanasoff moved to Maryland to work in the Naval Ordinance Laboratory, and Berry moved to California to work at the Consolidated Engineering Corporation. The ABC was left in the basement of a building at Iowa State. Its design was never patented, and it was dismantled several years later.

Mauchly, meanwhile, spoke to Atanasoff occasionally during the war. He told his friend he was creating a computer of his own, but one that was based on different principles than the ABC. That turned out to be untrue. In 1942, Mauchly convinced the army to build a top-secret, high-speed calculator that used vacuum tubes as switches. His proposal was largely based on Atanasoff's invention. However, Mauchly,

Early computers, such as the one shown here, were sometimes called "electronic brains."

working with electrical engineer J. Presper Eckert Jr., succeeded in building a machine that put the word "computer" into common usage and laid the foundation for the computer revolution that followed.

Mauchly and Eckert were on the faculty at the Moore School of Electronic Engineering at the University of Pennsylvania in Philadelphia. In 1943, the army granted them funds to build a machine to calculate artillery ballistic tables. New weapons were being developed and tested constantly. To keep up, the army needed tables showing how far and fast a newly invented bullet or shell could potentially travel. For weapons such as antiaircraft guns, the trajectory—the path that a projectile takes as it travels through

THE HUMAN COMPUTORS

The term computer once meant "a person who computes." It was applied to people who often worked in teams performing long, monotonous mathematical calculations. During World War II, when the U. S. Army needed hundreds of computers to calculate artillery ballistic tables, the term, spelled "computor," was typically applied to women who performed this task. Computor Jean "Betty" Batik recalled that female mathematicians were a rarity in the 1940s:

> I was the only woman mathematics major in my college [Moore School]. The jobs market was a big difficulty and we thought all we could do was teach school, and I definitely did not want to teach. My calculus teacher knew that and she received this recruiting notice from Aberdeen Proving Ground [a weapons testing facility in Maryland] looking for women math majors and she gave it to me. I applied for the job as a "computor"—my title was "computor"! Indeed all the women in that room were "computors": the label applied to female mathematicians long before it became synonymous with electronic boxes. It wasn't a very high-status name. It was a semiprofessional grade and most "computors" were women, while men were "mathematicians," professionals. But at least I wasn't teaching.[1]

According to Batik and others, John W. Mauchly called his invention the Electronic Numerical Integrator and Computer (ENIAC) as a way to emphasize that humans had been replaced with electronics.

1. Quoted in Mike Hally, *Electronic Brains*. Washington, DC: Joseph Henry, 2005, pp. 9–10.

space—needed to be calculated for every firing angle. This was extremely complicated. It took a mathematician about 40 hours to determine the trajectory for a single firing of a shell at a specific angle. To create useful firing tables, the military employed teams of mathematicians to calculate trajectories.

Each calculation took several weeks to complete. A faster, more efficient method was needed.

Mauchly, Eckert, and a team of 50 engineers and technical staff completed their work in November 1945. The result was the Electronic Numerical Integrator and Computer (ENIAC),

The ENIAC was huge, and it created a lot of heat with all its mechanical parts.

created to calculate firing tables. The machine cost $500,000 in 1945, the equivalent of $7 million in 2018. It weighed 30 tons (27.2 t) and covered three sides of a gigantic room. The machine contained thousands of dials and switches on 40 separate black panels that were 2 feet (0.6 m) wide and 8 feet (2.4 m) high. ENIAC was built into 49 cabinets housing nearly 18,000 vacuum tubes, all connected by miles of wiring. The vacuum tubes generated so much heat that a huge exhaust fan system was installed in the room's ceiling to keep the computer cool enough to function.

Despite its size and cost, ENIAC had less capability than a modern pocket calculator. It simply added, subtracted, multiplied, and divided numbers. However, to map bullet trajectories, large numbers had to be calculated thousands of times in many combinations, and ENIAC performed this task admirably. It could complete a ballistic trajectory in 1 minute, something that would take a mathematician 40 hours of work. Even more significant in the long run was that Mauchly and Eckert had devised complex methods whereby ENIAC could store data in memory banks. This meant that the next generation of computers could be based on the programs that engineers had devised for ENIAC.

The Arms Race Begins

By this time, the United States had dropped two atom bombs on Japan, which ended World War II, but the U.S. military still had a use for ENIAC. At the time, the United States was the only country with the power to level entire cities with nuclear weapons, as it had done in Japan. However, the Soviet Union was widely known to be developing its own atom bombs, which posed a threat to the United States.

The Soviet Union was a totalitarian Communist dictatorship. After World War II, the Soviets occupied Eastern Europe, and many Americans feared that the Communists would take over Western Europe and other nations throughout the world. U. S. government officials at the highest levels urgently wanted to build larger, more powerful nuclear weapons before the Soviets. The arms race between the United States and the Soviet Union had begun and would last more than 40 years, until the early 1990s.

To stay one step ahead of the Soviets, the American scientists who had built the atom bombs dropped on Japan now wanted to build a hydrogen bomb, or H-bomb, that would be 450 times more powerful. To design such a weapon, nuclear physicists needed a machine with the calculating power of ENIAC.

ENIAC Goes Public

While the plan to build an H-bomb was top secret, ENIAC was not. On February 25, 1946, scientists and reporters were given a tour and allowed to examine the world's only operating computer. Within days, articles about the gigantic thinking machine made international headlines. *TIME* maga-zine printed a glowing report about the room-sized calculator:

Its nimble electrons can add two num-bers of ten digits in 1/5000th of a sec-ond. New data can be fed into it at any stage of the process. If necessary, it can "remember" numbers and hold them for future use. An elaborate system of controls makes ENIAC so flexible that its inventors have given up looking for problems it cannot handle. There is plenty of work ahead for ENIAC, its inventors say. In nearly every science and every branch of engineering, there are proved principles which have lain dormant for years because their use required too much calculation.[3]

Scientists and reporters were not the only ones interested in the computer. Within 10 days of the machine's un-veiling, the government of the Soviet Union sent a purchase order to the Uni-versity of Pennsylvania, hoping to buy an ENIAC. Not surprisingly, the order was refused.

ENIAC was soon moved to the Ab-erdeen Proving Grounds in Maryland, where the military tested its weapons. That was home to the computer for sev-eral years until it was officially turned off on October 2, 1955. By then, the U.S. Air Force, in partnership with the International Business Machines (IBM) Corporation, was building computers that were even bigger than ENIAC and filled entire buildings.

Even as ENIAC was being moved, its inventors considered it obsolete and were already working on the next generation of calculating machines. According to technology historian Nathan Ensmenger,

I think very few people in 1946 had any idea that computing would be a commercial activity. The people who first used the ENIAC to solve signifi-cant problems were the U.S. Military ... and they had a very different image of what a computer would be used for. What Eckert and Mauchly ... brought to this was a vision of a computer as a commercial instrument. It was a vi-sion not shared by many people in the late 1940s and that made them very prophetic about the technology and where it was going.[4]

The UNIVAC

In 1946, Eckert and Mauchly founded the Eckert-Mauchly Computer Corpora-tion in Philadelphia. Instead of building one-of-a-kind machines like ENIAC, the men wanted to create a machine that could be mass produced and used for military, business, and scientific pur-poses. To fund this idea, they convinced the U.S. Census Bureau to grant them $300,000. Eckert and Mauchly set to work on the machine, choosing a name they hoped would demonstrate its wide appeal. They called it the Universal Au-tomatic Computer, or UNIVAC.

The Census Bureau was in dire need

On June 14, 1951, the UNIVAC I was dedicated after it had been delivered to the U.S. Census Bureau a few months earlier.

of an automatic calculating machine. The bureau is required by the Constitution to count the population of the United States every 10 years, and it received harsh criticism when the 1940 census took several years to complete. Faced with a growing postwar population, the bureau needed a powerful machine that could count and analyze the upcoming 1950 census data.

Over the next several years, the Eckert-Mauchly Computer Corporation sold contracts for UNIVAC to large firms that worked with numbers, including A. C. Nielsen, a marketing research firm, and Prudential, an insurance company. However, Eckert-Mauchly was continually running out of money to fund the project while paying its 134 employees. In 1950, financial desperation forced Eckert and Mauchly to sell their corporation to typewriter manufacturer Remington Rand.

Work continued on UNIVAC, however, and on March 31, 1951, the first commercially produced mainframe computer was delivered to the Census Bureau. While this was only a minor event in the news, the next year, UNIVAC was delivered to other customers

SINISTER LIGHTS

Duning the 1950s, the public's idea of what a computer looked like was formed by the UNIVAC. The large, black machine was covered with blinking lights. These lights, later called "blinkenlights" by computer historians, allowed engineers to monitor UNIVAC's various functions. While most people did not understand their purpose, blinkenlights became part of American culture through the movies. Whenever filmmakers wanted to show a sinister machine that might be used to blow up the world, they constructed black boxes modeled on the UNIVAC, complete with rows of blinkenlights. These menacing movie machines were seen in James Bond movies, often in secret laboratories run by heartless villains. Blinkenlights were also used in *War Games*, *Jurassic Park*, and other blockbuster films. Even in the 21st century, the lair of a villain frequently appears onscreen decorated with hundreds of blinkenlights.

Computers have been a part of pop culture for many years. Shown here is a scene set in a computer room in the 1967 film Billion Dollar Brain.

and became world-famous in the process. CBS News used a UNIVAC owned by the U. S. Atomic Energy Commission to accurately predict the 1952 presidential election, which was won by Dwight D. Eisenhower. The network's forecasts were so accurate, with a margin of error of less than 3 percent, that the country's three primary news networks used the computer to calculate predictions during the next general election.

An Important Transition

By the mid-1950s, the word UNIVAC was synonymous with "computer." The million-dollar machines were used by about 45 major American corporations and considered marvels of the modern age because they could perform more than 1,900 calculations per second. (By comparison, the average laptop today can make 4 billion calculations per second.)

While a UNIVAC was smaller than ENIAC, it could still fill a one-car garage and required constant maintenance. Each UNIVAC contained 5,200 vacuum tubes that burned out regularly. The tubes generated so much heat that a UNIVAC was filled with pipes that circulated cold water through the machine to keep the temperature down. The mixture of water and high-voltage electricity was very dangerous and required constant care by skilled technicians. This limited how many computers could be sold, as only large corporations could afford to purchase and maintain a UNIVAC.

Three physicists from Bell Telephone Laboratories in New Jersey solved the problem of the vacuum tubes in 1947, when John Bardeen, Walter H. Brattain, and William B. Shockley invented the transistor.

Transistors are small electronic devices that work in much the same way as vacuum tubes, but they are smaller, less fragile, and easier to make. Best of all, they produce less heat. The first transistor was 0.5 inch (1.27 cm) high. Once the design was perfected, transistors grew smaller every year, and, by the mid-1950s, they had shrunk to the size of a pencil eraser.

In 1956, the three Bell scientists shared a Nobel Prize in Physics for their work. Transistors revolutionized the world of electronics. The transistor radio was first introduced in 1955, and within just a few years, millions of people were listening to news, music, and sports on these handheld, battery-powered devices. Transistor radios made large, tube-filled radios obsolete, and they would do the same to UNIVAC.

The new radios used only a few transistors and were relatively easy to make. However, installing great numbers of transistors in large, complex computers was more problematic. The transistors had to be wired together with other electronic components in a time-consuming process involving soldering irons and magnifying glasses.

In September 1958, Jack Kilby,

working for Texas Instruments in Dallas, Texas, invented a device to replace individual transistors and their electronic components. Kilby realized that resistors and capacitors could be made from the same block of semiconductor material as transistors, eliminating the need to add capacitors and resistors manually. This allowed for smaller transistors, which could be made through an automated manufacturing process. Kilby called his invention an integrated circuit, or IC, saying his invention was "a body of semiconductor material … wherein all the components of the electronic circuit are completely integrated."[5]

In California, working independently of Kilby, Robert Noyce developed a better design for integrated circuits about six months later. Noyce, the founder of Fairchild Semiconductor, bonded all the

After the invention of transistors, small radios such as this one began replacing the large, clunky ones that had come before them.

components and transistors together on the surface of a circuit board made with the chemical element silicon. These silicon wafers, also called microchips, were superior to Kilby's integrated circuits because they were easier to mass produce. As a result, Kilby's chips were never widely used. However, after years of lawsuits between Texas Instruments and Fairchild, both Noyce and Kilby were given equal credit for inventing the IC. Noyce went on to found Intel, a semiconductor manufacturing company that still exists today, and the Northern California area he worked in became known as Silicon Valley.

Circuits in Space

The earliest computer built with integrated circuits was used to further humanity's understanding of outer space. In January 1958, space scientist James Van Allen designed an experiment to be conducted from the first American satellite, the unmanned *Explorer 1*. Van Allen was trying to measure the size and scope of the doughnut-shaped radiation belt that encircles Earth. However, the traditional measuring equipment aboard *Explorer 1* was overwhelmed by cosmic radiation and proved useless.

After the unsuccessful experiment, Van Allen contacted engineer Harvey Cragon at Texas Instruments. Cragon had recently built a primitive computing device made entirely from integrated circuits. Van Allen believed a similar machine could withstand the rigors of spaceflight while measuring extreme radiation. Cragon packed a box with integrated circuits, and it was placed aboard *Explorer 3*. Cragon's device worked well and was able to tally the radiation count, proving the existence of the Van Allen radiation belt. It was critical for the National Aeronautics and Space Administration (NASA) to understand the Van Allen belt in order to plan manned missions to the moon.

The 1401

Back on Earth, eight large companies saw promise and possible profits in computers built with integrated circuits. The machines, previously considered exotic and futuristic, were now viewed as having practical applications in business, the military, and scientific research. During the mid-1960s, electronics giants such as RCA, General Electric, Honeywell, Philco, and Raytheon began building and selling computers. Other companies, including Remington Rand, Burroughs, and Monroe, added computers to their widely used lines of business machines. The dominant force in the industry was IBM and its "Big Blue," a computer that came in a light blue metal cabinet.

IBM first solidified its position in 1959 with the introduction of the fully transistorized 1401 model. This was not just a mainframe computer, but also an integrated computer system. The 1401 mainframe relied on a fast, efficient central processing unit (CPU), an electronic circuit that can execute computer programs, and it used punch

Shown here is an IBM salesman in 1959. IBM is still known today as a leader in the computer industry.

cards. Punch cards were stiff paper cards with holes in certain positions that represented specific data. The computer could detect the pattern of the holes to retrieve this information. In an era before software, punch cards were used to create, store, and edit computer programs.

The 1401 also came with a printer that could print 600 lines of text per minute. The entire system sold for about $125,000 in 1960, or it could be leased from IBM for $2,500 (more than $21,000 today) a month. By 1962, about 2,000 businesses a year were leasing the 1401 system. It was used for everything from processing monthly utility bills to issuing payroll checks to managing freight car schedules. By the mid-1960s, the name IBM appeared on two-thirds of all computers in the United States.

A Space Computer

The 1401 was the first mass-produced, all-transistor business computer. NASA was interested in something similar to control the navigational functions of the Apollo spacecraft they were planning to send to the moon. The 1401 was too big and too heavy to fit inside the spacecraft, so NASA contacted scientists at the Massachusetts Institute of Technology (MIT) Instrumentation Laboratory to develop a solution. The agency's needs were daunting: The computer, potentially called the Apollo Guidance Computer (AGC), had to control a spaceship moving over 2,000 miles (3,200 km) per hour. It had to be able to land the ship safely within a few feet of a specific location on the moon's surface and then guide the lunar module to meet up with a command ship in lunar orbit. The computer was also required to do this perfectly on the first try, or the astronauts depending on it would die.

In the end, MIT succeeded, creating a 70-pound (31.8 kg) computer with 4,100 integrated circuits for just over $150,000. The computer had a 1 MHz (megahertz) processor and 1 K (kilobyte) of random-access memory (RAM). By contrast, typical computers today have thousands of times that processor speed and millions of times more RAM. Because of the primitive software, astronauts had to execute commands by performing more than 10,000 flawless keystrokes during the mission.

When *Apollo 11* landed on the moon on June 20, 1969, it was largely due to the AGC. The entire world took note. It was clear that computers made entirely with integrated circuits were the wave of the future—even if you were not going to the moon. Banks, airlines, railroads, insurance companies, automakers, and government agencies began using computers to keep track of their complex data.

For the average person at home, computers were still expensive and exotic machines that played little to no role in their daily lives, but that was about to change. Across the country, hundreds of college students began studying computers and imagining ways that everyone could use them. Their dreams would have a huge impact on the modern world.

CHAPTER TWO

THE ADVANCE OF COMPUTERS

Since 1927, *TIME* magazine has selected a "Person of the Year" for its year-end issue. According to the magazine, the choice is always a person who, "for better or for worse has done the most to influence the events of the year."[6] In 1982, the editors chose the personal computer, or PC, as "Machine of the Year." This was the first time in the magazine's history that a machine was chosen over the presidents, scientists, and other leaders who were traditionally seen as most influential. This choice reflected the huge advancements computers had made in the previous decade. According to *TIME*,

Now, thanks to the transistor and the silicon chip, the computer has been reduced so dramatically in both bulk and price that it is accessible to millions. In 1982 a cascade of computers beeped and blipped their way into the American office, the American school, the American home. The "information revolution" that futurists have long predicted has arrived, bringing with it the promise of dramatic changes in the way people live and work, perhaps even in the way they think. America will never be the same.[7]

Rapid Improvements

TIME's pronouncement came after there had been a surge in technological advancements throughout the 1960s and 1970s. With each passing year, new methods had been devised to increase the number of transistors that could be placed on a microchip, which in turn increased a computer's speed and power.

In 1966, Medium-Scale Integration (MSI) chips were developed that could hold up to 1,000 transistors. Jack Kilby, working at Texas Instruments with Jerry D. Merryman and James Van Tassel, used prototype MSI chips to build the world's first handheld calculator in 1967. The calculator was

Once the size of an entire room, by the 1980s, computers were about the size of a small television.

encased in an aluminum box, weighed nearly 3 pounds (1.4 kg), and had a small keyboard with 18 keys. While gigantic by modern standards, the calculator replaced an earlier generation of electronic calculators known as adding machines, comptometers, and numericators. These devices were about the size of old-fashioned typewriters, weighed nearly 55 pounds (25 kg), and

Hand-held calculators replaced the large machines, shown at bottom, from the 1960s.

THE TREND OF MOORE'S LAW

In 1965, Gorden E. Moore, a future co-founder of Intel, made a prediction that became known as Moore's Law. It stated that the number of transistors that could fit on an integrated circuit would double roughly every two years and would continue to do so into the future. This meant that the processing speed, memory capacity, and number of pixels on digital electronic devices would also continue to increase.

Moore's Law held up for decades, but by the 2010s, it was showing signs of slowing down. Computer parts have become so tiny that many experts believe that the laws of physics prevent them from getting even smaller.

had to be plugged into an electrical wall socket.

In 1969, Large-Scale Integration (LSI) chips, each containing 1,000 to 10,000 transistors, were developed. These chips made it possible for Texas Instruments to produce a smaller hand-held calculator. After partnering with the Japanese corporation Canon, Texas Instruments sold the Pocketronic calculator in 1970. The Pocketronic weighed about 1.8 pounds (0.8 kg), cost $395, and used paper tape rather than a visual display. It could perform basic arithmetic and algebraic math. Other companies such as Sanyo and Sharp soon began selling their own versions.

In 1972, after Texas Instruments invented a microprocessor—an IC with a central processing unit for basic operations—demand for calculators increased rapidly. The company's new chip was powerful, allowing the calculator to perform more functions while taking up much less space in the design.

By the mid-1970s, pocket calculators had replaced reliable old slide rules, and not just for accountants and engineering students—they were being used by everyone, for everyday purposes. Today, advanced microprocessors with thousands of transistors are found in nearly every electronic gadget.

West Coast Changes

While integrated circuits and microprocessors were undergoing changes, there were other developments in progress on the West Coast. At Stanford University in Palo Alto, California, two separate government-funded research labs were working on a number of futuristic goals, many of which centered on technologies that would eventually lead to the rise of the personal computer.

In 1963, at Stanford's Research Institute, Douglas Engelbart established the Augmented Human Intellectual Research Center, or ARC. Engelbart hoped to develop computers that would increase the power and abilities of human beings. On the other side of the campus,

LET'S PLAY *SPACEWAR*

Not all computer researchers were engaged in serious tasks. Computer programmer Stephen "Slug" Russell, who worked with John McCarthy at Stanford, invented the first primitive computer game, *Spacewar*, in 1962. Tech journalist John Markoff explained in his 2005 book *What the Dormouse Said*:

> [*Spacewar*] pitted two two-dimensional spaceships against each other on a background of stars. Pressing keys on the keyboard would move the ships on the display, and they could shoot tiny projectiles at each other. Spacewar was significant in that it was a classic collaborative hacking exercise, which would be cited as an early example of how open-source shared programs could be continuously improved by a group of volunteer programmers. For although Russell did the initial yeoman's work of creating the basic program, others had soon added lifelike constellations and a gravitational effect generated by a star placed in the center of the screen. ... A decade later a ... similar game, Computer Space, was developed by a young entrepreneur named Nolan Bushnell. Bushnell had come across Spacewar while he was a graduate student. ... Although Computer Space was a commercial flop, it was followed by Pong and the explosive growth of Bushnell's company, Atari.[1]

1. John Markoff, *What the Dormouse Said*. New York, NY: Viking, 2005, pp. 86–87.

at the Stanford Artificial Intelligence Laboratory, John McCarthy focused on building machines that could perform the tasks of the human brain, including speech, hearing, and sight.

Scientists who believed that computers could lead people into rich new worlds were a small minority at that time. There was another segment of society who suspected that computers were evil, part of a centralized bureaucracy led by IBM, with a goal of controlling humanity. Such doomsday scenarios, however, did not discourage those who wanted to harness the power of computers. According to tech journalist John Markoff in *What the Dormouse Said*, some of the leading researchers at Stanford computer labs "embraced [the computer] as a symbol of individual expression and liberation."[8] They represented the first generation of computer scientists—those who were determined to remake computers and turn them into tools of human growth and social progress.

"Dealing Lightning"

Engelbart's vision for computers to be used as personal information storage and retrieval systems for individuals was remarkably accurate. At ARC, he assembled a team of talented computer scientists, and by 1967, they had designed "an electronic office," a computer program that could integrate text with pictures. This simple concept is seen on millions of websites today, but it was a huge leap forward from the numbers and punch cards associated with the mainframe computers of the early 1960s.

While working on the electronic office, Engelbart's team invented an early version of the GUI, or graphical user interface. This consists of a pointing device and graphic icons used to control the functions of a computer. In order to operate the pointer on the user-friendly GUI, Engelbart's team invented several versions of the mouse, including the one commonly used today.

Engelbart's easy-to-use GUI operated differently from commercially available computers at the time. Other computers used the command-line interface (CLI) system, a method of programming that dated back to the 1950s. With CLI, users had to type lines of complicated text commands to get the computer to perform specific tasks. This required knowledgeable computer operators and had much more room for error.

The mouse and the GUI were part of what Engelbart called the oNLine System, or NLS. This system incorporated a mouse-driven cursor and multiple windows on a screen. The NLS also was the first to use hypertext, the system that uses hyperlinks to connect images, text, and other files on a network. Hyperlinks are used extensively on the web today, allowing users to access data on other pages by clicking on a highlighted picture or phrase.

In December 1968, Engelbart demonstrated the prototype electronic office at the Joint Computer Conference in San Francisco, California. He dazzled the 1,000 researchers and scientists in attendance when he used an ultramodern video machine, on loan from NASA, to project the display from his computer video terminal onto a 20-foot (6.1 m) screen. Operating the NLS from the stage, Engelbart described his inventions to the audience while waving his hands like a magician. During the demonstration, the faces of ARC staff members also appeared on the screen, linked through a homemade modem from the lab in Stanford 35 miles (56 km) away. His demonstration earned him a standing ovation. Although his system was too expensive to be practical, it still had a huge impact. Xerox computer designer Chuck Thacker said that it appeared as if Engelbart was "dealing lightning with both hands."[9]

Engelbart's demonstration was revolutionary in part because the NLS encouraged human interaction with the computer. As he asked the audience, "[How much value could you derive]

An early mouse invented in the 1960s by Douglas Engelbart and his team is shown here.

from a computer that was alive for you all day and was instantly responsive to every action you have?"[10]

Missing the Revolution

As Engelbart and his team were working on the NLS, Xerox Corporation was building the Xerox Palo Alto Research Center (PARC) to study digital technology and develop new computers. Xerox was one of the most profitable technology companies of the 1960s. It invented the world's first plain-paper copier in 1959, and these machines soon appeared in offices worldwide. Even today, the name Xerox is synonymous with photocopying, although the company did much more than that.

When PARC opened in 1970, Xerox hired the brightest scientists and students from ARC. During the next several years, ideas from ARC and NLS were incorporated into one of the earliest personal computers, the Xerox Alto. Engelbart was extremely bitter that Xerox stole his ideas and researchers, but his feelings made no difference to the forward march of technology. By the early 1970s, Engelbart and ARC were seen as irrelevant to corporate America.

The Alto computer was getting attention. It was the first computer designed to be operated by a single user and had many features that would eventually become standard. The Alto had a black-and-white monitor display on a tilt-and-swivel base and was operated through a detachable keyboard

While many of today's photocopiers only take up a small spot on a desk, they were once much larger, such as this one from the 1960s.

and a three-button mouse. Like modern computers, the mouse controlled the GUI. Users selected items from menus and clicked on icons to perform different functions. The Alto featured 128 KB of memory, expandable to 512 KB, and had a hard disk and a removable 2.5 MB (megabyte) memory cartridge. The computer also had a cable allowing it to be wired with other computers into a network, providing the first underpinnings of multiuser connections. With these features, the Alto could be used to run word processing and graphics programs and *Alto Trek*, one of the first network-based multiperson computer games.

Xerox never sold the Alto commercially—it would have cost roughly $40,000, around the average price of a new house in California at the time. However, Xerox did donate about 1,000 Altos to universities and similar institutions. One was even put to work in the information systems department of the White House. Ironically, Xerox, which was based in Rochester, New York, saw little value in the groundbreaking technology being developed in its West Coast office. The company's main business was photocopiers, and no one in management positions at Xerox expected the personal computer revolution. The company finally did begin marketing PCs in the mid-1980s, but it never successfully competed in the home computer market even though it had designed and built the first personal computer.

The Homebrew Computer Club

One person who was impressed with the Alto was a young computer hobbyist named Steven Jobs. Born in 1955, Jobs grew up in Cupertino, California, in the heart of the West Coast electronics industry. During high school, Jobs often attended student lectures at the technology corporation Hewlett-Packard (HP) and worked there during summer breaks. At HP, he met Stephen Wozniak, nicknamed Woz.

In 1975, Jobs and Wozniak began attending the Homebrew Computer Club, a group of 32 computer enthusiasts who met in a Silicon Valley garage. Homebrew members shared computer parts and tinkered with primitive circuit boards. The club was founded by Fred Moore, an activist against the Vietnam War. Moore was a member of the counterculture, people who resisted mainstream culture and believed in social change. He thought that computer networking and the sharing of software could be an important part of this movement. In 1984, Wozniak shared his memories of the club:

> It was in early 1975, and a lot of tech-type people would gather and trade integrated circuits back and forth. … Each session began with a "mapping period," when people would get up one by one and speak about some item of interest, a rumor, and have a discussion. Somebody would say, "I've got a new part," or somebody else would

say he had some new data. ... During the "random access period" that followed, you would wander outside and find people trading devices or information and helping each other.[11]

In early 1976, Wozniak built a computer with mail-order electronic parts and joined with Jobs to sell it. They called it the Apple 1 (later known as Apple I). For years, people wondered where the name came from. In Wozniak's 2006 memoir, *iWoz: Computer Geek to Cult Icon*, he wrote about the origin of the name:

It was a couple of weeks later when we came up with a name for the partnership. I remember I was driving Steve Jobs back from the airport along Highway 85. Steve was coming back from a visit to Oregon to a place he called an "apple orchard." It was actually some kind of commune. Steve suggested a name—Apple Computer. The first comment out of my mouth was, "What about Apple Records?" This was (and still is) the Beatles-owned record label. We both tried to come up with technical-sounding names that were better, but we couldn't think of any good ones. Apple was so much better, better than any other name we could think of.[12]

Wozniak built the Apple I to be a game machine for computer hobbyists. Although the computer was nothing more than a bare circuit board with no case, screen, or keyboard, it contained ports so that a keyboard could be added and a television could be hooked up as a monitor. Jobs and Wozniak built about 200 of the machines, which they sold for $666.66 (Wozniak liked the repeating numbers.) from the garage belonging to Jobs's parents.

On April 1, 1976, the two men founded Apple Computer. In early 1977, with $250,000 supplied by an investor, Apple was incorporated, and in April of that year, the company introduced the Apple II at the West Coast Computer Faire. Unlike the Apple I, sold in a wooden box, the Apple II, with its plastic case, had a sleek, professional look. It featured an integrated keyboard and sound, and it could run VisiCalc, the first spreadsheet program for personal computers. In its second year of production, Apple II could run the word processing program WordStar and a database management system called dBase.

Apple II was one of the first personal computers ever sold, and it is credited with starting the home computing revolution. With no competition in the personal computer market, Apple sales grew from $2.7 million in 1977 to $7.8 million in 1978.

In 1979, Jobs wanted to make the Apple II easier to use by removing the command line interface that controlled the machine. He had read about the GUI system used on the Alto and believed it could replace the Apple's CLI. He arranged to get a tour of the Xerox

The Apple II looked like a television merged with a typewriter, and it sparked a consumer craze that few could have predicted.

PARC facility and was shown several amazing things, including 100 Altos wired together in a computer network. The thing that excited Jobs the most was the GUI, with its multiple open windows, hypertext, icons, and menus on the screen. While the display was primitive and flawed, Jobs later recalled that within 10 minutes of viewing the GUI, he knew that all computers would someday work in a similar manner. Incredibly, the manager of PARC seemed unaware of what Xerox possessed. When Jobs later requested a demonstration for Apple's entire programming team, they were given a 90-minute presentation of an Alto machine running a GUI. Jobs realized that he had found a truly user-friendly computer that anyone could operate.

Jobs was known for his brash business style, and he offered Xerox the opportunity to invest $1 million in his fledgling company. He also asked that Apple developers be able to study and adapt the Alto. Xerox was not planning on selling the Alto and did not think the public would be interested in it, so they agreed to the deal. Apple first used the Alto GUI on its model computer called Lisa. In return, Xerox received 100,000 shares of Apple's company stock for $10 each.

When Apple made a public stock offering six months later, Xerox sold its stock for a hefty profit. However, the technology they had given to Apple was priceless. In 1980, four years after Jobs and Wozniak were selling computers out of a garage, Apple sales reached an astounding $177 million. A year after that, the company was worth more than $1 billion. Although Jobs died from cancer in 2011, Apple continues to be a major force in the market. In 2018, the company's value surpassed $1 trillion, with the average share price more than $225.

Keeping It BASIC

The success story of Jobs and Wozniak has an uncanny parallel in the suburbs of Seattle, Washington. Like the founders of Apple, William "Bill" Gates III and Paul Allen were high school friends who shared a passion for early computer technology, and they both became very wealthy after obtaining technology from a major corporation that did not recognize its value.

Gates and Allen first became interested in computers in high school. In 1975, when Gates was 20, he read a story in the magazine *Popular Electronics* about a computer called the Altair 8800, which was sold as a mail-order kit. Hobbyists enjoyed the challenge of simply assembling the pieces of the machine, although it did not do much. Once the kit was completed, a user could toggle the Altair's 16 switches to correspond with an operating code that came with the device. By hitting the enter switch, the process was repeated several times. If this tedious programming was properly performed—which it often was not— the machine's red lights would blink in patterns.

The Altair did contain one revolutionary new development, however. It was sold with the Intel 8080, an advanced microprocessor. The Intel 8080 in the Altair could execute 290,000 instructions per second and had 64 KB of memory. This allowed the computer to run the programming language called BASIC, or Beginner's All-purpose Symbolic Instruction Code. As its name implies, BASIC is designed for beginners, with an interactive programming language.

It has clear, friendly error messages and built-in defenses that prevent beginners from harming the computer's operating system. BASIC is also versatile enough that experts can add extra features to it.

Gates and Allen recognized that the Altair, with its Intel microprocessor and BASIC programming, was the first computer with the speed, power, and efficiency to be programmed to run multiple software applications. They contacted the Altair's manufacturer,

This Altair 8800 is kept at the Computer History Museum in Mountain View, California.

Micro Instrumentation and Telemetry Systems (MITS), and offered to demonstrate the enhanced BASIC programming language they had devised.

MITS was very interested in Gates's and Allen's proposal. In July 1975, the two men founded a company they called Micro-Soft (the hyphen was soon dropped) to develop and sell the software program they wrote with the BASIC programming language. Instead of selling the software outright to MITS, Gates decided to license it. This meant that anyone who purchased an Altair would have to pay for the right to use the advanced software operating system Gates and Allen had designed. With this new operating system, the Altair was in great demand. Within months, the company sold several thousand kits for $439 each.

Gates dropped out of college to run his growing computer software business, and within a few years, Microsoft BASIC programming was being incorporated into home computers. An even bigger success came in 1981 when the company was hired by IBM to develop a disc operating system, or DOS, for its upcoming line of personal computers. DOS software manages and coordinates basic activities performed by a computer.

Rather than design a brand-new DOS system, Microsoft modified an existing system called QDOS, the "Quick and Dirty Operating System," written by Tim Paterson of Seattle Computer Products. Gates bought the rights for the system for $50,000 and renamed it MS-DOS. Once he provided the operating system to IBM, Gates talked the giant corporation into letting Microsoft retain the right to license MS-DOS whether it was sold on IBM computers or any other brand. With the MS-DOS system available to anyone who wanted to pay for it, dozens of companies, including Compaq, Dell, Gateway, and Toshiba, began selling computers based on IBM hardware. These clones hurt IBM's business in the personal computer market, but the large demand for MS-DOS made Gates and Allen billionaires.

Enter the Mac

By 1985, MS-DOS had transformed and gained a new look as Microsoft Windows. The software incorporated a GUI and was sold with millions of IBM clones, now simply called PCs, that were dominating the home computer market.

Apple, meanwhile, refused to allow other companies to clone its products or unique operating systems. The company attempted to stay ahead of the competition with an innovative new product, the Macintosh computer.

The Macintosh, or Mac, was different because of its easy to-use GUI, which was considered superior to Windows, especially for graphic and art applications. Macs could run MacPaint and MacDraw software, which allowed graphic artists, for the first time, to create type fonts in various sizes and manipulate and organize text, photos, and images on a computer monitor. However, Macs cost more than PCs, and Apple's share of the computer market fell to about 15 percent by the late 1980s. By 2017, Apple manufactured just under 13 percent of all computers sold in the United States, but its users remained fiercely loyal to the brand.

Time to Play

During the late 1970s and early 1980s, the computer evolved from a mail-order hobby machine to a hot consumer product. The first computer store, ComputerLand, opened in Hayward, California, in 1976 and by 1982, had grown into a nationwide chain with 600 stores. By that time, computers were the basis of a worldwide information revolution. Software programs were helping people do everything from managing investments to learning foreign languages. However, the fastest area of computer growth was not knowledge—it was gaming.

In 1982, 20 corporations sold 250 different games, collectively earning

THE EVOLUTION OF GAMING

No matter how computer gaming has evolved over the past several decades, one thing is clear: It remains hugely popular. By 2014, a quarter of the world's entire population was playing a computer game. While the first games were cassettes inserted into the computer, followed by compact discs, almost 80 percent of today's games are delivered digitally.

The format of these games has changed dramatically, but so have the games themselves. Although they started with fairly simple graphics, they became far more advanced. Today, the graphics are often so realistic that they appear almost like a film with live actors. Instead of being single-player, many games are "massively multiplayer online role-playing games," or MMRPGs, that allow players from all over the world form online teams to battle monsters, enemy armies, and other obstacles. Teams strategize together despite language and time zone barriers. Many educators believe gaming has helped young players improve everything from their spelling and grammar to their understanding of world geography.

In addition to playing games, thousands of players also attend annual video game conventions. In 2018, the largest conventions were Dreamhack in Sweden and the Electronic Entertainment Expo, or E3, in Los Angeles, California. More than 69,000 people attended E3, and more than 3,000 new gaming products were showcased.

roughly $2 billion. This was astounding for an industry that had barely existed five years earlier. The growth of computer gaming drove computer sales. In the early 1980s, more than half of all personal computers were purchased solely for playing games. Sociologists debated whether computer games were educational, but as Otto Friedrich pointed out in a 1983 article in *TIME*, "Probably the most important effect of these games ... is that they have brought ... the computer into millions of homes and convinced millions of people that it is both pleasant and easy to operate, what computer buffs call 'user friendly.'"[13]

By the mid-1980s, the image of the personal computer was changing almost daily. No longer was it just for high-tech government agencies and big corporations. No longer was it considered a "centralized brain" or a sinister threat. It was a tool—and one that was becoming increasingly user-friendly. Computers continued to get faster and smaller and, in the process, less intimidating for people to try. They were revolutionizing the world, and the implications were more than almost anyone, from a curious consumer to a skillful computer engineer, could have imagined.

CHAPTER THREE

HITCHING A RIDE ON THE INFORMATION HIGHWAY

One day in the 1970s, Dale Heath-erington was sitting at the dining room table in his friend Dennis Hayes's home. Together, they were brainstorming an idea for a new company. With a pen and a few napkins, they drew their ideas for ways to get computers to connect with other computers using telephone lines. Not long after, the two men opened D. C. Hayes Associates and began selling their exciting new invention: the Smartmodem. This small appliance was designed to convert a computer's digital signals into analog signals via telephone lines, making it possible for people to exchange messages, pictures, and other digital information through a series of electronic buzzes, beeps, and pings.

In addition to converting the signals, the Smartmodem answered incoming calls from other computers, dialed numbers to initiate calls, and hung up when the call was complete.

When the Smartmodem initially went on sale for $300, few customers were interested. The only people excited by the device were computer hobbyists who understood how the Smartmodem worked and how it had the potential to change the way people exchanged information.

The Smartmodem was designed to connect to Apple IIs and most other home computers available at the time. By the early 1980s, as personal computer sales were exploding, people came to understand the value of the Hayes modem. Computer-savvy people realized that with a computer, a modem, and a common phone jack, they could log in to what was called the Telenet. This telephone network allowed them to link their home computers to computers at other locations, which then gave them access to a variety of programs and data such as library catalogs. Computer users could also access FTP, or file transfer protocol, sites. FTP sites allowed users to transfer files between their systems and other systems. It was often difficult and time-consuming to do this, but these connections were the first step toward today's internet.

Staying Ahead of the Soviets

Hayes's Smartmodem was not the first modem, but it was four times faster than older modems devised by the U.S. Air Force in the 1950s. Military modems were part of the air defense system called SAGE (Semi-Automatic Ground Environment), built to track and intercept Soviet bombers. The military modems connected SAGE's computers to computers at dozens of airbases, radar sites, and command centers. While SAGE was technically the first computer network, its use was limited to high-security personnel.

The internet of today also began as a military project in the 1950s. After World War II, many people were extremely nervous about the growing power of the Soviet Union. This period of tensions was known as the Cold War. Americans built bomb shelters in their backyards and practiced emergency drills at school and at work to prepare for a nuclear attack. Tensions increased in 1957 when the Soviets sent the first satellite, called *Sputnik 1*, into space. Many people mistakenly believed the Soviets could use satellites such as *Sputnik* to drop atomic bombs on American cities. In addition, many Americans believed it was a national embarrassment that the Soviets had managed to beat the United States in the race to space.

With the Soviets establishing themselves as military and scientific leaders, U.S. president Dwight D. Eisenhower felt that it was crucial for America to catch up. For the United States to be superior, Eisenhower felt that an information revolution was essential. To fund projects that would bring cutting-edge technology to the U.S. military, the president created the Advanced Research Projects Agency (ARPA) on February 7, 1958.

ARPA's directive was to finance scientific research with a strong focus on rocketry, nuclear power, computers, and electronics. After the agency was created, universities across the country received ARPA grants to set up a variety of research programs. At the time, few people were studying computer science, but ARPA spurred demand for researchers in the field.

Sending Data

Leonard Kleinrock was one of the people attracted to computing because of ARPA. Kleinrock, who had a degree in electrical engineering, was a graduate student at MIT. He had previously worked in the school's Lincoln Laboratory, where SAGE was developed. While studying for his doctorate degree in computer science, Kleinrock decided to research computer communications, a field that he believed

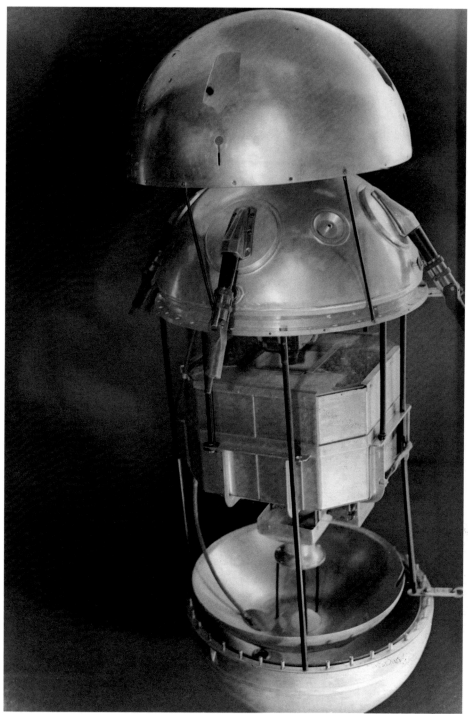

During the Space Race of the 1950s, the Soviet Union took the first critical step forward by launching the satellite Sputnik 1 *(shown here) into orbit.*

could revolutionize information sharing. In 1962, Kleinrock finished his doctoral thesis, which established a mathematical theory called "packet switching." This digital networking communications method was important to the development of the internet.

Packet switching is a way in which data is organized and electronically transmitted in blocks with fixed lengths called packets. The packets can be switched, or routed and distributed, with precision, accuracy, efficiency, and control. When packet switching takes place, data is separated into packets at the beginning of a transmission. The packets flow through a variety of network pathways, and if one path is disrupted, the block of digital data is rerouted onto another path. When the packets reach their destination, the computer on the other end of the transmission reassembles the information into usable data.

Packet switching was an improvement over the networking system called circuit switching used by telephone companies at that time. With circuit switching, during exceptionally busy times, circuits could become jammed with too much information, and messages could not get through. Packet switching resolved this issue, making it possible today for internet users to send and receive everything from a quick email to a full-length movie without delay.

Two Visionaries

Kleinrock was not the only person at MIT using ARPA grants to explore computerized information sharing. In 1962, the psychologist and computer scientist J. C. R. Licklider became the head researcher at an ARPA-funded project at MIT called the Information Processing Techniques Office (IPTO). Years before the invention of small, personal computers, Licklider was a visionary who imagined the digital world as it exists today, where people and computers could work together.

Licklider envisioned that this social interaction would take place over computer networks much like today's internet. In a 1962 paper, *On-Line Man-Computer Communication*, Licklider conceived of what he called the Intergalactic Computer Network, or Galactic Network, in which everyone on Earth would be interconnected through computers, accessing programs and data from any site, anywhere.

Licklider left the IPTO in 1965, and Robert Taylor, another computer scientist with the organization, took over as its leader. At the time, Taylor also worked for the Department of Defense, where he used three different computer terminals for different purposes. One was hooked into a network at MIT; another to the University of California, Berkeley; and the third into a computer at Rand Corporation. However, the computers were not connected to one another. Drawing on the theory of the Galactic Network, Taylor

*Long before other people,
J. C. R. Licklider envisioned
a future where people
routinely used computers.*

decided to link the computers into a single, common network. Commenting on the idea in a 2008 interview, Taylor stated,

> *When I had this idea about building a network—this was in 1966—it was kind of an "Aha" idea, a "Eureka!" idea. I went over to [ARPA Director] Charlie Herzfeld's office and told him about it. And he pretty much instantly made a budget change within his agency and took a million dollars away from one of his other offices and gave it to me to get started. It took about 20 minutes.*[14]

"I… o…"

Taylor hired Larry Roberts, a 29-year-old electrical engineer, to help develop a computer communications network better than the ones then used by the military. Roberts and others quickly succeeded in getting two computers to communicate. They were hooked up on what was called a wide area network, or WAN. One computer was in California, the other in Massachusetts. However, the telephone lines used for the experiment used circuit switching, which made the communications slow and inaccurate.

Taylor realized that packet switching would solve this problem. Working with researchers at a small Massachusetts consulting firm called Bolt, Beranek and Newman (BBN), Taylor began to develop a network

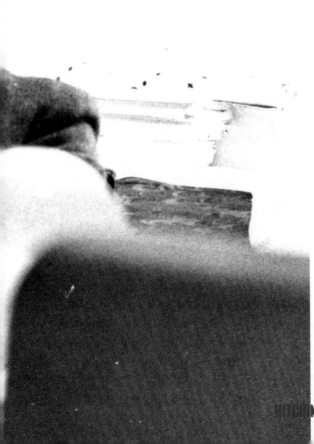

Leonard Kleinrock is shown here with the first IMP.

made up of large and powerful computers known as Interface Message Processors, or IMPs (now called routers), that were connected to each other through lines leased from the phone company.

The first IMP was installed at the University of California, Los Angeles (UCLA), where Kleinrock was a faculty member. The machine, made by Honeywell, was called a minicomputer.

By September 1969, the network, now called the Advanced Research Projects Agency Network (ARPANET), was ready for testing. Four computer nodes were hooked into a network at UCLA; Stanford Research Institute; the University of California, Santa Barbara; and the University of Utah. On October 29, 1969, at 10:30 p.m., Charley Kline, a UCLA student programmer supervised by Kleinrock, attempted to send the first message over the ARPANET. The message was to be a single word: "login." However, the system crashed after the first two letters, "l" and "o," were sent. An hour later, the system was back up, and the complete word was sent to a computer at Stanford. Within weeks, the ARPANET was fully functioning. However, as Kleinrock has pointed out, this was not big news outside a few computer labs:

We didn't even have a camera or a tape recorder or a written record of that event. I mean, who *noticed? Nobody did. Nineteen sixty-nine was quite a year. Man on the moon. Woodstock. Mets won the World Series. Charles Manson starts killing these people here in Los Angeles. And the Internet was born. Well, the first four everybody knew about. Nobody knew about the Internet.*[15]

The general public might not have cared about the obscure ARPANET project, but Kleinrock's news release, with the headline "UCLA to Be First Station in Nationwide Computer Network," proved to be prophetic. During the years that followed, the ARPANET expanded to colleges and government research centers across the country. In the release, Kleinrock predicted that someday computers would be in homes and offices across the country, linked together by providers similar to electric and telephone companies.

Welcome Email

Another important step in the information revolution took place in 1972. Engineer Ray Tomlinson, one of the developers of the ARPANET, was working with two software programs at BBN. One was CPYNET, or Copynet, which was designed to transfer files between computers. The other program was SNDMSG, or Send Message, a memo program that allowed computer users to leave messages for one another on the same computer.

Colleges and universities, such as the one shown here, were places where students could explore the growing field of computer science.

Tomlinson was struck with the idea that the two programs could be combined to send messages from one computer to another. By slightly changing—or hacking—the programs so they worked together, Tomlinson invented electronic mail, or email.

Tomlinson understood that this type of mail also needed an address, just as traditional mail used. Communications had to be sent not only to an individual but also to a specific computer on the network. Tomlinson came up with the idea of writing email addresses in two

HACKERS THEN AND NOW

Some of the students, faculty, and researchers at MIT who worked on the internet believed computers were serious tools that could be used to generate information. Others, known as hackers, saw computers and software as complex toys that could be manipulated to play games or perform clever tricks simply for fun. These people enjoyed learning the details of programs to expand on their capabilities. Early hackers were generally members of the counterculture who believed that software should be created and shared freely. However, in the 1980s, the term hacker was misused by the media to describe people who created computer viruses or illegally broke into computer systems, often to commit crimes. Since then, the term has been used to refer to people with sinister motives.

Today, hacking is one of the biggest threats people face from using their computers. As computer use has expanded, so has the risk of having information stolen, changed, or used for dangerous purposes. Experts believe there is a hacker attack every 39 seconds in the United States, with one-third of Americans being impacted. In a particularly dramatic example, in 2016, Russian operatives hacked into various U.S. computers in an attempt to influence the presidential election.

At the IBM Security Summit in 2015, Ginni Rometty, IBM's company president and chairman, stated, "We believe that data is the phenomenon of our time. It is the world's new natural resource. It is the new basis of competitive advantage, and it is transforming every profession and industry. If all of this is true—even inevitable—then cyber crime, by definition, is the greatest threat to every profession, every industry, every company in the world."[1]

1. Steve Morgan, "IBM's CEO on Hackers: 'Cyber Crime is the Greatest Threat to Every Company in the World," *Forbes*, Nov. 24, 2015. www.forbes.com/sites/stevemorgan/2015/11/24/ibms-ceo-on-hackers-cyber-crime-is-the-greatest-threat-to-every-company-in-the-world/#64d8e54a73f0

parts: one representing the individual user, and the other the network. These were joined by the "@," or "at," sign, such as user@computer. Despite the enormous potential of email, the first message was neither profound nor brilliant. Tomlinson simply dragged his finger across the keyboard, creating a nonsensical jumble of letters, and sent it to himself.

Early email was certainly not as effective as it is today. Users could not reply to, save, or delete messages. Tomlinson worked hard to make the system better, and as he did, email's popularity increased. Eighteen months after it was invented, email made up more than three-quarters of all computer traffic on the ARPANET.

The amazing growth of email took many ARPA pioneers by surprise. This was an unplanned consequence of the ARPANET project, as internet developer Bob Kahn later commented:

ARPA never would have funded a computer network in order to facilitate email. The telephone was a quite serviceable device for person-to-person communication. But once [email] came into existence, it had tremendous benefits: overcoming the obstacles of time zones, messaging multiple recipients, transferring materials with messages, simple collegial and friendly contacts.[16]

Tomlinson's email program was a "killer app"—one that is so useful and desirable it broadly increases the number of people using and buying computers. After Tomlinson's first message, email only continued to grow, eventually spreading through government offices, universities, corporate offices, and the homes of ordinary people. In 2017, 269 billion emails were sent and received, and by 2022, experts believe that number will be more than 333 billion!

Network of Networks

As the ARPANET and email use expanded, Robert Metcalf, who worked at the Xerox PARC, devised an efficient method to link computers, printers, and other devices into local area networks, or LANs. Working with a team of inventors, Metcalf developed the Ethernet between 1973 and 1975.

The original Ethernet allowed communication over a single cable shared by all devices on the network. Once a computer was attached to the Ethernet cable, it could communicate with any other attached device. It also had access to information stored on the other computers. Metcalf left Xerox in 1979, but he worked to convince major computer manufacturers to use the Ethernet as a standard method of connecting computers to LANs. Today, Ethernet connections are at the center of all computer networks.

Through its early years, the ARPANET worked well because all the routers were built by the same company using the same design. This ensured connection reliability because all links in the network were compatible. By the mid-1970s, however, many different types of computers were used as nodes. Getting each one to function smoothly with the routers was difficult and time-consuming, and system crashes were common.

Another connection problem was based on the growing number of incompatible packet-switching networks that were developed by government agencies, universities, and corporations. One such network, the Atlantic Packet Satellite Network, or SATnet, sent and received data through satellite transmissions. At the University of Hawaii, researchers developed the AlohaNet, which used radio signals for computer communications. Unfortunately, none of these systems could "talk" with one another.

Kahn and researcher Vinton Cerf decided to tackle the incompatibility problem. They wanted to construct a universal network that would function with all computers. The network would be based on a standard set of computer communication instructions, called protocols. The protocols would have to work on a wide variety of computers and routers so they could connect, communicate, and transfer data.

Kahn and Cerf coined the term

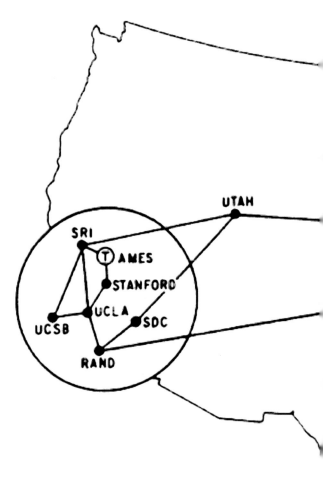

"internetworking" to describe their new system. It was not a single computer network, but a network of networks all interlinked through packet switching. The word "internetworking" was soon shortened to internet.

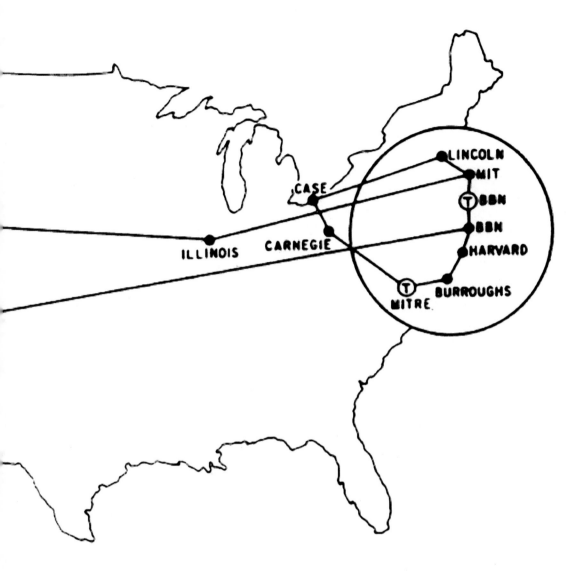

This map shows how the ARPANET worked by connecting communication centers.

It was based on a system of standard-ized network communications rules called transmission control protocol (TCP) and internet protocol (IP). Later, the two terms were combined as TCP/IP.

Across the Miles

In July 1977, Cerf set up a complex test for the TCP/IP system. Using funds from the Department of Defense, he organized a team of operators working in locations across the

United States and Europe. Cerf began the test by transmitting data to BBN headquarters from a van driving on a San Francisco freeway. The message then went to Norway and London, through SATnet, and back to the United States in West Virginia. From there, Cerf's message traveled on to England, Sweden, Germany, and Italy before finally returning to California. By that time, it had successfully traveled 94,000 miles (151,278 km) across the globe through the ARPANET, the SATnet, landlines, and other packet networks.

The TCP/IP system was 25 times faster than the ARPANET and worked so efficiently that it was chosen as the preferred military protocol in 1980. By 1982, the board of directors that administered the ARPANET decided that all of the network's sites would have to convert to TCP/IP protocols as soon as possible. In order to force the switch, the old system was turned off for one day in June 1982. Then, it was shut off for two days several months later. Finally, the old protocols were permanently shut off on January 1, 1983. The ARPANET had transformed into the internet.

The internet was used mainly by government institutions and schools until 1989, when the federal government opened the network to commercial traffic. The first company to profit from this change was MCI Mail, the first commercial email service available to home computer users.

Other companies, such as OnTyme, Telemail, and CompuServe quickly understood the internet's potential. They built network access sites that subscribers paid about $6 an hour to use. These early systems, in addition to being expensive, required users to type line commands, which limited their use to people with computer skills.

The situation changed in October 1989 when America Online (AOL) became the first company to offer its own software to internet users. The software, which was designed to be user-friendly, proved wildly popular, and the company's customer base grew from about 10,000 customers in 1989 to more than 1 million in 1994. In 1997, the company bought rival CompuServe and soon after, Netscape. By 2000, it was the nation's biggest internet provider.

By that time, millions of devices, from personal laptops to supercomputers at the Department of Defense, were connected to the internet, earning Cerf the nickname "Father of the Internet" because his work had successfully linked millions of people.

Among the Millions

Imagine trying to find information in a library where a million books have been thrown into a pile on the floor. That is similar to how difficult it was to access the millions of files in cyberspace during the late 1980s. Users had to figure out where a file was stored, and then input a series of complicated commands in order to access it. This problem was particularly vexing to British scientist Tim Berners-Lee, who worked at CERN, a large physics laboratory in Geneva, Switzerland. Since 1980, Berners-Lee had worked to make computers easier to use, and he wanted to devise methods to help his colleagues locate computer files.

Berners-Lee solved this problem by using the concept of hypertext, first developed in the 1960s by Douglas Engelbart. Hypertext embeds codes in documents that appear as highlighted text on a computer monitor. When users click on a hypertext link, they are taken to the site where the document is stored. In 1989, Berners-Lee refined hypertext to create hypertext markup language (HTML), a coding system that could identify not only text but also pictures and sounds.

Working with data systems engineer Robert Cailliau, Berners-Lee also created the hypertext transfer protocol (HTTP), a set of networking rules that allows HTML files to move between computers on the internet. Another innovation, the universal resource location (URL), provides a method to identify every unique document on the internet. Before URLs were invented, computer users had to type in long strings of numbers, letters, and symbols to find documents on other computers. With URLs, such as http://www.google.com, web addresses became easier to remember.

Berners-Lee later commented on his inventions: "The power of a hypertext link is that it can link to absolutely anything. That's the fundamental concept. The fundamental idea was anything which was out there somewhere sitting on a computer disk where that computer was attached to a network, you ought to be able to give it an address, you ought to be able to link to it."[17]

HTML software and HTTP and URL protocols formed the backbone of what Berners-Lee referred to as the World Wide Web. The software was made available to the public for free in August 1991. While some people at CERN wanted to trademark the words *World Wide Web*, Berners-Lee fought the idea. As Cailliau recalled, "I was talking about that with Tim one day, and he looked at me, and I could see that he wasn't enthusiastic. He said, 'Robert, do you want to be rich?' I thought, Well, it helps, no? He apparently didn't care about that. What he cared about was to make sure that the thing would work, that it would just be there for everybody."[18]

Computer programmers quickly recognized the power of the World Wide Web and used it to combine words, pictures, and sounds to create attractive, interactive web pages and websites.

Time to Browse

Two years after the World Wide Web was made available to the public, the

Mosaic browser was developed by Marc Andreessen and Eric Bina. A browser is a software application that allows users to display and interact with text, images, videos, music, games, and other information displayed on web pages. Mosaic, which later became Netscape Navigator, was easy to use and contributed to the widespread popularity of the World Wide Web. In 1995, Microsoft introduced a rival browser, Internet Explorer, which quickly dominated the market. Internet Explorer faced competition when the Firefox browser came online in 2002, followed by Safari in 2003. In 2008, the technology company Google, already known for its powerful search engine, introduced the Google Chrome browser. Chrome is now used by more people than any other browser.

By the mid-1990s, the web was growing by 2,300 percent a year

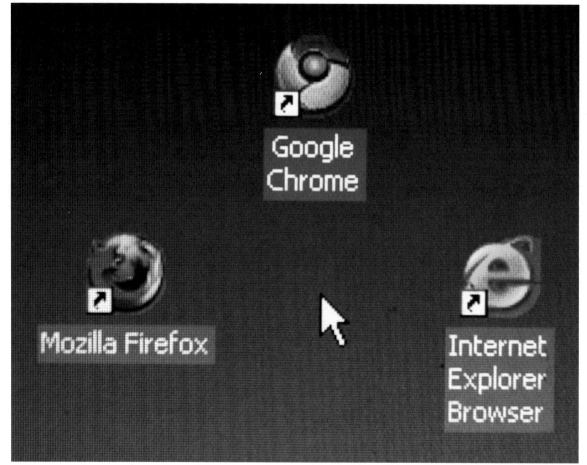

Several companies, including Mozilla, Google, and Microsoft, compete for business with different browser software.

and changing the very nature of human communications. Commenting on these developments, computer scientist Lawrence H. Landweber stated in 2008, "The World Wide Web turns the Internet into a repository, the largest repository of information and knowledge that's ever existed."[19]

Decades have passed since the invention of packet switching, GUI, and computer chips. Since then, the melding of hypertext, networks, and the personal computer have combined to produce something that is much bigger and more important than the sum of its parts. Of course, it has not always been a smooth journey, and there have been skeptics and critics along the way. Journalist Mike Royko once stated, "It's been my policy to view the internet not as an 'information highway,' but as an electronic asylum filled with babbling loonies."[20]

Nonetheless, most people today agree that the internet has transformed the world. As Kenneth Cukier, senior editor at *The Economist* magazine said, "In terms of the spread of knowledge, the past two decades have been as revolutionary as when early man harnessed fire."[21]

CHAPTER FOUR

OPEN TO EVERYONE

As the last decade of the 20th century began, millions of files with information on almost every academic subject possible were on the country's computers. Except to people in the military, government, or academia, however, those files were mostly inaccessible. As the world rushed forward to the new millennium, that began to change. Companies selling everything from software to pet supplies saw the potential of appealing to computer users. One of those people was a hedge fund analyst who was certain he understood the needs and wants of the average internet user and wanted to start a business to appeal to them. His name was Jeff Bezos.

The Arrival of Amazon

Bezos started by making a list of 20 different products that he thought college-educated men in their 30s might be interested in purchasing online. (At the time, 82 percent of internet users were male.) Then, in 1994, Bezos quit his job in New York City and drove across the country to Seattle, Washington, where he drew up a business plan for a company called Amazon.com.

Bezos launched Amazon in 1995, and today it is the country's most popular store. It has more than 310 million active customers and sells products in virtually every consumer category, from computers and electronics to home goods and sporting equipment. In the beginning, however, Amazon sold just one thing: books. Bezos explained to *Vanity Fair*,

I picked books because books are very unusual in one respect. And that is that there are more items in the book category than there are items in any other category, by far. There are millions of different books active and in print. I was also looking for

Amazon founder Jeff Bezos saw a consumer need
and fulfilled it beyond anyone's expectations.

something that you could only do on the Web. And having a bookstore with universal selection is only possible on the Web. You could never do it with a paper catalogue. The paper catalogue would be the size of dozens of New York City phone books, and it would be out of date the second you printed it. And you could never do it in a physical store. You know, the largest book superstores carry about 150,000 titles, and there aren't very many that big.[22]

Within a few years, Amazon.com was the biggest bookstore in the world. Bezos had correctly predicted that customers would appreciate the combination of commerce and computers that gave them a wide selection of products and the convenience of shopping from their own homes. Since its early days, Amazon has moved far beyond books, offering more than 3 billion different products around the world. Many items come from third-party sellers, and sales in 2017 reached $178 billion.

In 2005, the site began offering a new service called Amazon Prime. Customers who paid the annual fee to receive this service received free two-day shipping on many products. In spring 2018, Bezos stated that more than 100 million people had signed up for Prime.

In an unusual move for an internet-based business, in early 2018, Amazon also opened its first brick-and-mortar store in Seattle. Described as "a kind of grocery store without cashiers or a checkout line,"[23] Amazon Go uses cameras and sensors to recognize customers and track what they put in their carts and then bills them on their smartphones.

The immense popularity of Amazon had unintended consequences. Amazon sold books at lower prices than most bookstores, and many independent booksellers were unable to compete with the internet giant. Since the late 1990s, thousands of small bookstores have gone out of business, meaning that communities have also lost places that hosted author readings, educational lectures, and other events—something Amazon does not do. Amazon's strength eventually impacted large bookstore chains too. By 2011, companies such as B. Dalton's, Waldenbooks, and Borders had all closed their doors. Even as Amazon promoted choice and convenience for its customers, it made it impossible for them to browse the shelves of old-fashioned bookstores in their neighborhoods.

Searching the Internet

The growth of the internet did not just impact readers. It changed the way people learned entirely. Suddenly, information that was previously found only in books was now freely and easily available online. This was due to the search engines that came to dominate the internet in the 1990s.

As the number of websites grew from 130 in 1993 to more than 600,000 in 1996, the search engine became a necessary tool for finding facts. As technology consultant J. R. Okin wrote in *The Information Revolution* in 2005, "The Web is an information space— something that is superimposed on the Internet that provides a means to locate, dispense, and interconnect information."[24] Search engines such as Google, Yahoo!, and Bing work by connecting words entered by a user to a database of web pages. The engine then produces a list of hypertext URLs with summaries of contents that are relevant to the query.

One of the most popular early search engines was actually invented for purposes other than searching the web. Managers at Digital Equipment Corporation (DEC) were looking for ways to demonstrate the power of their extremely fast Alpha microprocessor. In 1994, to show it off, researchers loaded the entire contents of the web onto a single computer and built a software program that could quickly access, search, and index the information on the individual pages. This experiment resulted in the birth of the search engine AltaVista, launched on December 15, 1995. On its first day of operation, the AltaVista site received 300,000 visits. Within a year, AltaVista had answered more than 4 billion queries, and by 1997, the search engine was receiving more than 25 million hits a day.

AltaVista dominated the web for a time, but it was then challenged by another search engine created by David Filo and Jerry Yang, two electrical engineering graduate students at Stanford. When Filo and Yang launched the search site in April 1994, they called it "Jerry and David's Guide to the World Wide Web," but it was soon renamed Yahoo!—a word the inventors say was chosen as a joke because it refers to a person who is rude, unsophisticated, and uncouth. By the end of its first year, Yahoo! had received more than 1 million hits. By 2000, the price of Yahoo! stock had skyrocketed to $118 a share, and the company founded by two graduate students was worth nearly as much as IBM.

Many stories about Filo and Yang focus on the incredible sums of money they made in the second half of the 1990s, but there was a good reason investors believed the company was so valuable. Yahoo! forever changed the way people access and use information. It offered users email accounts, chat networks, notepads, calendars, and address books. It also provided a variety of information services that covered news, sports, finance, music, movies, and games.

With these features, for the first time, web users could go to a single site to check the weather, make travel plans, look for a job, find housing, learn about a product, and even find a person with whom to go on

Yahoo! was the first search engine visited by many computer users.

a date. Businesses were also able to take advantage of the Yahoo! network. Companies now had the tools to communicate with customers and with each other, providing links for business meetings, product launches, and other information.

Search engines have continued to develop since the days of AltaVista and Yahoo!. In 1998, Google was established and quickly grew to be the most-used search engine in the world. In just the month of July 2018, Google processed 11.74 billion search queries. Google has become such a part of daily life for many people that is it often used as a verb. When information is needed, the solution for many people is to "Google it!"

Growing—and Shrinking

As the internet expanded, the computers needed to access it actually began to shrink in size. Apple's first laptop computer, the PowerBook 140, was released in 1991. The PowerBook was the first computer built with a palm rest, trackball mouse, and other features that eventually became standard on laptops. The first PowerBook weighed 6.8 pounds (3 kg), had 2 MB of RAM, and cost $3,200, but computers became lighter, more powerful, and cheaper as the decade progressed.

The success of the PowerBook inspired other manufacturers to begin making laptops. The popular IBM ThinkPad was released in 1992. Three years later, Microsoft introduced

A WHOLE NEW VOCABULARY

Part of the computing revolution meant learning the new language that went along with it. Mice were not just little rodents anymore. Bytes were not just things taken out of food, but a way to measure storage space. Bugs and viruses did not just make people sick—they infected computers as well. The internet's creation led to more terms. "Surfing the net" came to mean looking around online without a specific goal in mind. While "Spam" is a brand of processed meat, because of the internet, it also refers to unwanted emails.

The internet has even been responsible for creating new words. For example, in 2011, it added the terms "woot" (an exclamation of excitement) and "noob" (a new person who is unsure about what to do). In addition, the internet has also led to numerous acronyms for expressions. LOL (laughing out loud), IMO (in my opinion), and SMH (shaking my head) are used online and have also merged into students' writing. Teachers report that such abbreviations have become so common that they pop up in students' essays and reports.

the Windows 95 operating system (OS), which quickly became a standard feature on all IBM clone laptops. The same year, CD-ROM drives, high-quality Intel Pentium processors, and floppy disk drives became available on nearly all laptops. Throughout the rest of the decade, laptops continued to improve with faster processors, better batteries, hard drives that had more storage space, and color visual displays. Since then, laptops have continued to evolve. Screen sizes can be small or oversized, depending on whether users want something compact and easy to carry around or a large display that is good for graphics or gaming. Floppy disk drives have been replaced with thumb drives (also called flash drives), and most laptops have batteries that last several hours.

As laptops have become more advanced and more affordable, their sales have surpassed desktop computers. The convenience of a relatively light computer (typically 5 pounds or less) that can be taken anywhere is hard to beat. In 2017, 97.8 million desktops were sold, compared to more than

Ten years after introducing its first laptop, Apple released the titanium PowerBook G4 in 2001.

161 million laptops. Experts predict that by 2022, that number will grow to more than 165 million, even as the overall number of computers sold is expected to decrease.

A Pivotal Event

The internet had its first major impact on politics during the late 1990s, when Bill Clinton was president. Clinton became involved in a scandal when it was discovered he had had an affair with a White House intern, Monica Lewinsky. The details quickly spread—and the internet was one of the main ways these details reached people.

On January 17, 1998, Hollywood gossip columnist Matt Drudge broke the Lewinsky story on his website, the Drudge Report. The headline read: "Newsweek Kills Story on White House Intern: 23-Year-Old, Sex Relationship with President."[25] As a result of the attention given to the story on the Drudge Report, it was finally covered by the *Washington Post* newspaper four days later. Other mainstream media outlets also began reporting the story. Political opponents of Clinton used the scandal to call for the president's impeachment, which took place in December 1998. (Clinton was acquitted by the Senate in February 1999, so he was able to stay in his job as president.) The role played by online reporting in calling attention to the story proved to be a pivotal event in internet history.

Drudge was a product of the internet age. He was a troubled teen whose father bought him a computer to keep him busy and out of trouble. After working at a series of minimum-wage jobs, Drudge was hired in 1996 as a clerk in the CBS gift shop in Hollywood. There, he heard gossip about various celebrities and began publishing the stories in an email newsletter that he sent to subscribers for $10 a year. A conservative Republican, he started the Drudge Report website in 1997 to broaden his base of email subscribers. A year later, he reported on the Lewinsky scandal, scooping reporters at major media outlets. As CNN reporter Gregg Russell stated the week the story broke, "Welcome to journalism in the Internet Age: an age when a 30-year-old former CBS gift-shop clerk like Drudge, armed with a computer and a modem, can wield nearly as much power as a network executive producer or the editor of *The New York Times*."[26]

The Lewinsky scandal brought hundreds of thousands of readers to Drudge's website, but not everyone thought he deserved the attention. Critics accused Drudge of printing inaccurate, sensationalized information while pushing a conservative agenda aimed at destroying Clinton. However, even in 1998, Drudge foresaw a revolution in the way news was covered, predicting that ordinary citizens would play a role in finding

The political scandal involving President Bill Clinton and intern Monica Lewinsky began with online reporting and spread from there.

and reporting news: "You don't get a license to report in America. We have a First Amendment freedom. In the future, there will be 300 million reporters with websites and email accounts. I'm looking forward to it. I think the monopolization of news really screwed up a lot of things."[27]

Moving On

When Drudge broke the Lewinsky scandal, the White House had just started building its first website, but the impeachment controversy demonstrated the power of online politics for the first time.

In 1998, major political parties and most individual politicians were not yet using the web to raise funds and reach voters. Still, liberal computer entrepreneurs Joan Blades and Wes Boyd understood that they could use the internet to oppose conservatives like Drudge. Like Drudge, they began with email. As Blades recalled,

Wes and I were in a Chinese restaurant hearing yet another table talking about the insanity of having our government obsessed with the [Lewinsky] scandal when there were other, important things the government might be doing. And we wrote a one-sentence petition: Congress must immediately censure the president and move on to pressing issues facing the nation.[28]

Blades and Boyd sent out the email petition to several hundred people and asked them to pass it along. In modern terms, the email petition went viral. Within a few days, more than half a million people had signed it. According to Blades, "This was in '98. I don't think anything like that had ever happened before on the Internet. ... So we had the proverbial tiger by the tail."[29]

The overwhelming response to their petition led Blades and Boyd to found MoveOn.org, a political action committee (PAC). PACs are groups founded specifically to elect or defeat political candidates, and MoveOn.org quickly attracted over 3.2 million members. The PAC was credited with helping Democrats win a congressional majority in 2006. It was also credited with helping Barack Obama win the White House in 2008 and again in 2012.

The success of MoveOn.org inspired thousands of people with all kinds of political views to create their own political websites. Major political parties and individual politicians got involved and set up their own websites. For the first time, voters could closely follow the progress of legislation as bills wound their way through the House and Senate. They could contact their representatives by email or sign petitions supporting or opposing various bills. This was a significantly faster form of activism than the days when people sent letters to their representatives through the postal service. Today, there are countless websites and news outlets devoted to politics, reaching millions of followers.

The Advent of Streaming

As sources of up-to-the-minute information, political websites created competition for newspapers and magazines, but other traditional media were threatened by the internet. In 1995, RealNetworks, Inc., founded by former Microsoft executive Rob Glaser, released RealAudio player, a free, downloadable software program that brought audio-on-demand to the web. The first broadcast, in September 1995, was a baseball game between the New York Yankees and the Seattle Mariners. The *Los Angeles Times* wrote, "The game was played in New York and carried on a local radio in Seattle, but internet users from Los Angeles to Lagos were able to hear the play-by-play by using freely available software called RealAudio."[30]

At the time, few people had high-speed broadband internet connections, and wireless was unavailable. Most users connected to the web through low-speed modems attached to phone lines. Anyone

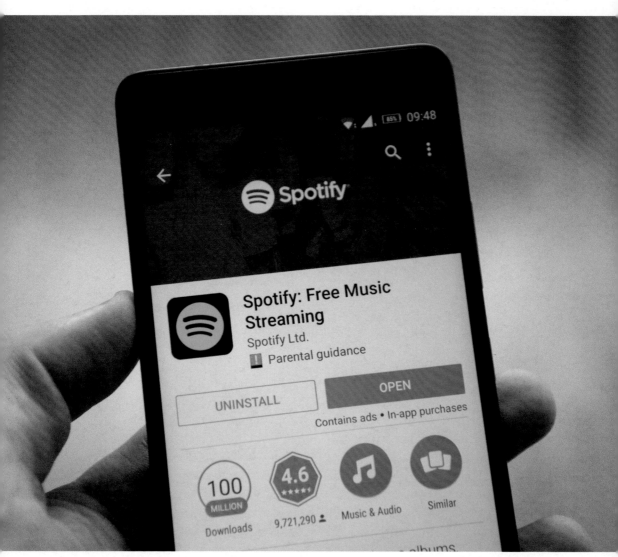

Streaming music services, such as Pandora and Spotify, reach users all over the world.

trying to download a complete file of a 10-minute radio program could spend more than an hour trying to do it—and that depended on the modem staying connected, which it often did not. RealAudio engineers solved this problem by using a new technique called streaming audio. That meant a person could begin to hear a song or broadcast even after only a small portion had been downloaded.

It did not take long for RealAudio to change the way millions of people listened to music. Established radio stations took advantage of the internet and used it to broadcast their programs to a worldwide market. However, the new technology allowed almost anyone to set up an inexpensive radio station. Amateur disc jockeys could create programs and stream them live on the internet, or they could create the files, archive—or store—them on a site, and then allow users to access them on-demand. These stations featured a wide variety of programming, including alternative rock, traditional and world music, and opinion and educational programs not typically heard on mainstream radio.

Unlike traditional radio stations, web-based stations were not required to follow the costly and complicated rules set forth by the Federal Communications Commission (FCC). Stations could broadcast from anywhere in the world without the need for expensive transmitters. One of the earliest internet radio stations, 'A'

Net Station (ANET) demonstrated this concept when founder George Maat broadcast music and commentary from Antarctica.

In early 1997, RealNetworks made RealVideo players available for free. Like the audio player, RealVideo allowed streaming of video clips. In May 1997, the electronic dance band Depeche Mode participated in one of the first online video chats. In January 1998, President Clinton gave the first State of the Union speech that was broadcast not only on television but on RealVideo as well.

Since the beginning of the 21st century, even more free music players have become available on the internet. Free players such MusicBee, AIMP, and MediaMonkey keep music organized and easily accessible. Companies such as Pandora and Spotify also offer vast libraries of free music to listen to online, and, with a paid membership, everything is completely commercial-free. As phones and computers have developed the ability to stream music, the compact disc (CD) industry—a huge business in 2000—has collapsed. Many music companies have stopped selling them altogether.

The "Dot-Com" Bubble

During the second half of the 1990s, stock values of internet companies soared, helping fuel a technology, or "dot-com" boom. Some investors became extremely wealthy, but the boom did not last. By 2001, it was clear that simply having a web address or being a technology company was not an automatic guarantee of success. Many companies failed, taking their financial backers down with them. Investors became much more cautious when it came to online businesses. It was clear that internet and technology companies were here to stay, but the artificial bubble of the late 1990s had burst.

Before the dot-com bust, however, dozens of web companies became household names. They found success by freely sharing information while allowing users to contribute to online conversations about every topic imaginable. While the web was invented and developed by mathematical and scientific geniuses, it served to increase the intelligence level of the public at large. As web use grew from thousands of people to billions, questions previously answered with "I don't know" were answered with "Let me look it up" instead. Learning, sharing, understanding, and responding to information would never be the same again—and it all had happened in less than a decade.

A NEW ERA OF INSTANT INFORMATION

The last decade has brought so many changes, updates, and advances in the use of the internet that it is almost impossible to keep up with the innovations. Cell phones and computers have improved rapidly, with each generation of these devices offering features that were unheard of only a matter of years ago. Thanks to the use of fiber optic cables—cables made of thin strands of glass—data now moves via light pulses rather than electric currents, making it possible to carry virtually unlimited amounts of information. The internet also took a huge step forward when telephone modems were replaced by broadband connections, allowing users to download audio and video files in minutes instead of hours. In 1996, wireless internet connections, or Wi-Fi, were developed. Today, people can go online from wherever they are, whether it is their home, a public coffee shop, or even their car.

Another important change occurred when, instead of purchasing software programs, consumers began to simply download them directly from the internet. Software cassettes or game discs were replaced by a click of the mouse and a direct download to the computer. Consumers are even moving away from some programs altogether. For example, many people used to buy word processing programs, such as Microsoft Word. Now, many people choose to use a free online system, such as Google Docs, which also allows multiple users to simultaneously edit the same document.

Blog and Vlog

Matt Drudge once predicted that the United States would have 300 million reporters—and he was partially correct. Although only a tiny fraction of the country's population are professional journalists, the internet has made it possible for anyone with a computer to share their ideas and opinions. In the 1980s, people on the internet formed discussion groups to talk about particular topics or share their news and lives with others, but this practice did not really take off until the launch of a program called Blogger.

With it, people could now write about whatever they wanted in their own online journal, or blog. (The word is short for "weblog," which comes from creating a "log" of thoughts or experiences on the web.) Followers can read, comment on, and share those thoughts with others. Experts estimate that almost 32 million people will be blogging in 2020. Popular topics include fashion, food, travel, music, lifestyle, entertainment, finances, do-it-yourself projects, and fitness. Some bloggers make a living writing their blogs, thanks to their sponsors

Streaming made buying discs of games obsolete, putting an end to many stores that specialized in selling these products.

The Huffington Post *is one of the millions of blogs that keep readers current on everything from politics to parenting.*

and advertisers. For example, in 2017, the most popular blog on the internet was the *Huffington Post*. Through its banners and digital ads, it brought in $14 million per month.

Being Social

While some people spend their time online sharing their opinions and expertise on a variety of topics, many are just there to chat about life with their friends and family on social media sites.

The social media movement began in 2002 in Mountain View, California, when former Netscape engineer Jonathan Abrams created a website called Friendster. Abrams explained why he started the site:

Before Friendster, people who had a profile online were either a geek or somebody on a dating site, and the sites did have a stigma. People would sign up for traditional dating services like Match.com and then hope all their friends never saw their profile. I wanted to flip that upside down and create a service where you would actually deliberately invite your friends to use it with you. One of the analogies was that it was like a cocktail party or a nightclub.[31]

While Friendster started the social networking trend, it was quickly eclipsed by Facebook, which launched in 2004. Today, Facebook is the biggest social media site on the internet, with more than 2 billion users worldwide. (If Facebook was its own country, it would have a larger population than China!) Other popular social media include Snapchat, Instagram, and Twitter. Every minute, more than 30 million posts are shared on Facebook and 350,000 tweets are posted on Twitter. Research shows that 52 trillion words are written every day on social media—the equivalent of more than 500 million books.

Besides keeping people in touch, social networks provide other useful information to the public. The site LinkedIn, for example, is a professional networking site launched in May 2003. With more than 562 million users worldwide,

LinkedIn allows members to create business contacts, search for jobs, and find potential clients.

In some cases, social networks have allowed people to protest government oppression. For example, Facebook became quite popular after it launched in Colombia, where the government censors the press and other speech. According to Facebook founder Mark Zuckerberg, "the first thing that a lot

THE SMARTEST PHONE

Your smartphone will not take you to the moon—but not because it does not have enough "smarts." The cell phones that most people carry actually have more computing power than the computers used in most NASA spaceships. Today's phones are amazing—and although it is easy to take them for granted, they have come a long way in just a few short years. In the process, they have made many items people once used routinely obsolete. With a smartphone, it is no longer necessary to own an atlas, camera, audio or video recorder, wristwatch, alarm clock, calculator, flashlight, calendar, or TV—not to mention a separate landline telephone. All those things and more now fit in the palm of your hand!

CENSORING THE FREEDOM OF SPEECH

While millions of new blog posts go up every day in the United States, people in many other countries do not have the same freedoms as Americans. In China, for example, speech is closely monitored by the government, and social media posts, website content, blogs, and even text messages can be censored. The Chinese government has made it clear that blogs about fashion or entertainment are acceptable, but posting controversial or negative comments about the government or politics is strictly off limits.

Other countries that have restrictions on what their people can post online include Iran and North Korea. In these countries, bloggers must register with the government in order to have their material accessible on the internet.

Increase in Total Internet Users: 2000 vs. 2018

■ 804x ■ 250-500x ■ 100x-250x ■ 50x-100x ■ 10x-50x ■ 5x-10x ■ 2.5x-5x 1.5x-2.5

The number of internet users worldwide has exploded in less than two decades, as shown on this map.

Facebook moved its company headquarters to Menlo Park, California, in 2011 and named the campus's main thoroughfare "Hacker Way."

of people started doing was ... using the decentralized communication medium [of Facebook] to start organizing and protesting against the armies there."[32]

The Wonder of Wiki

Facebook and other social networking sites could not exist without the user-generated content that allows people to build online communities.

Another modern success based on collective contributions is the online encyclopedia Wikipedia.

In the past, people bought books or CDs of encyclopedias. Wikipedia is a perfect example of how things have changed. Launched in 2001, the site is based on a powerful piece of technology called a wiki that allows anyone to make an entry to a page or to edit content supplied by other

Wikipedia is a free encyclopedia that invites users to edit, add, and comment on online articles.

users. This means that Wikipedia is constantly edited and updated by the public. As of late 2018, Wikipedia had 29 million articles written by users and more than 34 million contributors called "Wikipedians."

The accuracy of information on Wikipedia is sometimes called into question, but the nature of the online encyclopedia makes it very difficult to fact-check since an average of 1,500 to 2,000 new articles are added daily—and about 1,000 are deleted. However, incorrect articles are often quickly fixed by others. Such persistent revisions keep content fresh and up-to-date in a way that old-style encyclopedias cannot.

Millions of people have come to rely on Wikipedia, which is one of the top 10 destinations on the internet. However, Wikipedia cofounder Jimmy Wales views the site as more than a place where people can go to find facts: "I don't think of my work as technological innovation. ... Primarily what we are doing is social innovation, finding ways for people to work together in social communities online and figuring out what social rules and norms are helpful for people to create healthy and productive communities."[33]

The Risks of the Internet

With more websites published every day, the internet has become the world's biggest repository of information. It is virtually impossible for the human brain to comprehend the true amount of information on the web. After all, experts estimate that in a single day:

- 656 million tweets are posted on Twitter
- more than 4 million hours of video are uploaded
- 4.3 billion Facebook messages are posted
- 5.2 billion Google searches are made

Although the internet is full of knowledge and connection, it is not without some risks. All these messages, thoughts, comments, and articles can lead to a case of information overload, where a person feels overwhelmed and even paralyzed by too many details and facts. It can also result in a condition known as "digital addiction." With this type of addiction, people find that the desire to use their phones, browse the internet, or check social media sites interferes with their lives.

Another issue the digital age has introduced is the loss of personal privacy. It is frighteningly easy for people to forget that what they post online does not simply disappear after a period of time. Even non-public activity—like using a credit card to buy something online—creates a digital signature that stays, even if the person later deletes information. There is always a risk that someone else will find private information that was never intended to be shared. Email addresses, home addresses, telephone numbers, birthdays, credit card and bank account numbers, social security numbers, hometowns, employment history, and many other details can be gathered and used against people. Some hackers will take those details to run up charges on credit cards, while others may even steal a person's identity completely, not only spending their money but committing other acts under that person's name. In many instances, personal information that was entered into a website in order to become a member, play a game, or make a purchase is sold to companies so they can try and sell additional products to people.

A painful reminder of how vulnerable people can be to companies gathering data about them came in 2018. Christopher Wylie was an employee for the British political consulting firm Cambridge Analytica, which mined and analyzed large amounts data on behalf of its clients. Wylie spoke publicly about the company's software program, which had collected the data of tens of millions of Facebook users over the past few years and then used it for political purposes. Among the company's clients was the campaign

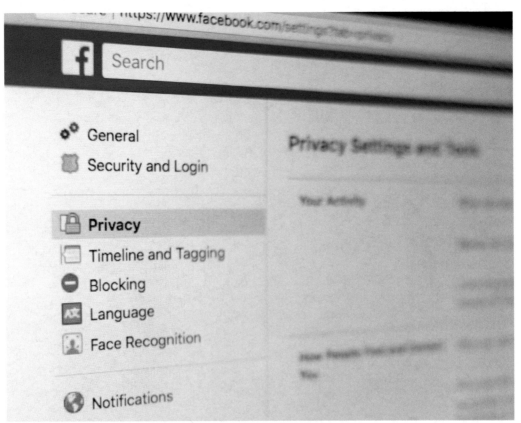

Easy access to online information makes life simpler but also brings threats to privacy and security.

of Donald Trump, who ran for U.S. president—and was ultimately elected—in 2016. "We exploited Facebook to harvest millions of people's profiles," Wylie stated. "And built models to exploit what we knew about them and target their inner demons. That was the basis the entire company was built on."[34]

When Facebook found out about the security breach, however, it did not alert its members about what had happened. Instead, it merely asked the company to delete the data it had gathered. Following that, more people at Cambridge Analytica were recorded admitting that they had interfered not only in the 2016 U.S. presidential election, but also in electoral campaigns worldwide. In May 2018, the company shut down, and many people were wiser about the risks of putting information on the internet and the need for better, stronger privacy policies.

Staying Neutral

In 2015, the Federal Communications

A March 2018 protest against Cambridge Analytica was led by Christopher Wylie in Parliament Square in England.

Commission (FCC) approved regulations that would require internet service providers (ISPs) to give equal access to all websites on the internet, no matter what type of information they contained, where they came from, or how big or small the site was. The concept of "net neutrality" meant that a huge commercial website like Amazon or Google would be treated the same as a small business's website or a personal blog. People who wanted to view a smaller site would not be required to wait longer for it to load into their browser simply because it was less popular.

In 2017, these regulations were repealed in a controversial vote by the FCC. This now meant that ISPs could give priority to certain sites and make others slower and less accessible. They could favor certain sources or types of information. There had been some instances of this happening in the past, and opponents of the deregulation feared it opened the door to it happening again. Many communications and information companies have merged into large conglomerates, and as a result, many people suspected that these mega-companies would try to promote their own content with customers in an effort to make more money and would throttle the efforts of their competitors. This would have been illegal with net neutrality in place.

Supporters of the deregulation, however, pointed out that the internet had been unregulated throughout most of its existence. Simply repealing the regulations did not mean that companies would alter their service to restrict some types of information and promote others. If they did, these proponents argued, consumers could simply choose another provider. Free-market competition would take care of any problems. Many people do not have a choice between providers, however, which could prevent the free market from acting to their benefit.

The Birth of "Fake News"

In 2016, after Donald Trump was elected president of the United States, a new term became popular: "fake news." Fake news describes information that has been intentionally created and then spread through the media in the hope of deceiving or misleading people into believing things that are unproven or even outright lies. Trump accused news outlets, including CNN and the *New York Times*, of skewing the news against him because they did not like him or his political policies. He labeled much of their coverage as "fake news."

Most of the news Trump objected to showed him in a negative light, but in many cases, it had been researched and documented and was not actually false. However, there was plenty of "fake news" that really was fake. Politics and partisanship played a big role. Some people disagreed so strongly with other political viewpoints that they invented false information and stories to made their opponents look bad. International politics was also part of the problem. U.S. intelligence analysts discovered that during and after the 2016 election, Russia created fake news stories and circulated them to American audiences in an effort to sway voters and increase division and hostility among American citizens. Other countries also had problems with the distribution of fake news, as well as with politicians claiming news was fake if they did not like it—even if the reports were accurate.

The idea that journalists, reporters, and other media experts were deliberately lying to the public is upsetting to many people, and the issue of fake news is a dangerous one. It puts doubt into the minds of many citizens about whether they are reading or hearing the truth of what

SPOTTING FAKE NEWS

Determining whether news is true or not is not always easy. National Public Radio (NPR) suggests that people pay close attention to the domain and URL of the site the news is coming from. The "About Us" section on a news outlet can offer more information about the outlet's history, mission, and standards. Readers should also watch for melodramatic words that signal personal bias or a desire to appeal to someone's emotions rather than reporting facts. Quotes in the story should be from professionals, experts, or people closely connected to the story. In general, reporters are expected to use the names of their sources unless they explain why that is not possible.

happened. In addition, people tend to want to believe reports that align with their personal opinions and values. If those reports are false, it hurts their ability to consider real facts and make appropriate decisions.

In the past, most news was in print, and it was easy to look at the covers of publications and recognize which were legitimate news sources and which were tabloids full of unreliable information. With the advent of computers and smartphones, however, this has changed. As Steven Rosenbaum stated in *Forbes* magazine,

> But the shift from print to the mobile web mushes together all media into a similar looking stream of posts … no one really knows the difference between the Denver Post and the Denver Guardian. Hint, one is an established newspaper with writers, editors, and fact checking. The other is a fake news site … with stories totally made up out of his active imagination and published from his home in the suburbs of L.A. … Creating an algorithm that can define what Fake is is taking on a game of whack-a-mole that's sure to fail.[35]

In addition to fake news, another disturbing development was the increase of hate speech on the internet. Some people targeted minority groups, such as African Americans or Jewish people, and posted hateful and sometimes threatening speech about them on social media sites or other platforms. In response, some sites revoked the accounts this speech came from, and some web hosting companies refused to host these types of websites. Others, however, said that individuals had the right to voice their opinions, even if the company did not agree with those views. In addition, it is difficult to monitor every account or website, so many instances of hate speech stayed active on the internet. If one account was canceled, a user could simply set up another one.

In the past, mass information was controlled by a relatively small number of people. The internet changed that, making it possible for anyone with a computer to create and distribute information. With that, however, came a greater responsibility for people to understand how to evaluate and use information.

The internet also revolutionized how people relate to one another. It made everything more immediate, from ordering dinner to catching up with the news. At the same time, it made distance less important and connection more possible. Some say it brought people closer together, giving them a fast, efficient way to communicate across the globe. Others say it pushed people apart, replacing the expressions of human faces with the pixels of digital screens. There are obvious advantages to the information revolution as well as tough questions about how it will ultimately impact society. For those questions, humans still have to answer, "I don't know."

Notes

Introduction:
The End of "I Don't Know"

1. Umberto Eco, "Vegetal and Mineral Memory: The Future of Books,"
   Umberto Eco Readers, November 18, 2007. umbertoecoreaders.blogspot.
   com/2007/11/vegetal-and-mineral-memory-future-of.html.

Chapter One:
A Calculated Approach

2. "Literary Paternity Test: Who Fathered the Computer?," NPR,
   November 20, 2010. www.npr.org/2010/11/20/131469545/literary-
   paternity-test-who-fathered-the-computer.

3. "Eniac," *TIME*, February 25, 1946. www.time.com/time/magazine/
   article/0,9171,852728,00.html?promoid=googlep.

4. Quoted in Mike Hally, *Electronic Brains*. Washington, DC: Joseph Henry,
   2005, pp. 21–22.

5. Quoted in Brian Winston, *Media Technology and Society: A History; From the
   Telegraph to the Internet*. London: Routledge, 1999, p. 221.

Chapter Two:
The Advance of Computers

6. *Person of the Year: 75th Anniversary Celebration*. New York, NY: Time Books,
   2002, p. 1.

7. Otto Friedrich, "The Computer," *TIME*, January 4, 1983. www.time.com/
   time/subscriber/personoftheyear/archive/stories/1982.html.

8. John Markoff, *What the Dormouse Said*. New York, NY: Viking, 2005, p. xii.

9. Quoted in Markoff, *What the Dormouse Said*, p. 148.

10. Quoted in Markoff, *What the Dormouse Said*, p. 150.

11. Quoted in Steve Ditlea, "Digital Deli: The Comprehensive, User-Lovable Menu of Computer Lore, Culture, Lifestyles and Fancy," Atari Archives, 2008. www.atariarchives.org/deli/homebrew_and_how_the_apple.php.

12. Steve Rivkin, "How Did Apple Computer Get its Brand Name?," Branding Strategy Insider, November 17, 2011. www.brandingstrategyinsider. com/2011/11/how-did-apple-computer-get-its-brand-name.html.

13. Friedrich, "The Computer."

Chapter Three:
Hitching a Ride on the Information Highway

14. Quoted in Keenan Mayo and Peter Newcomb, "How the Web Was Won: An Oral History of the Internet," *Vanity Fair*, July 2008. find.galegroup.com/ gtx/infomark.do?&contentSet=IACDocuments&type=retrieve&tab ID=T003&prodId=ITOF&docId=A180901850&source=gale&userGroup Name=itsbtrial&version=1.0.

15. Quoted in Mayo and Newcomb, "How the Web Was Won."

16. Quoted in Stephen Segaller, *Nerds 2.0.1*. New York, NY: TV Books, 1998, p. 105.

17. Quoted in Segaller, *Nerds 2.0.1*, p. 289.

18. Quoted in Mayo and Newcomb, "How the Web Was Won."

19. Quoted in Mayo and Newcomb, "How the Web Was Won."

20. Sam Parker, "16 of the Wisest Things Anyone Ever Said about the Internet," BuzzFeed, May 15, 2013. www.buzzfeed.com/samjparker/quotes-about-the-internet.

21. Pew Research Center, "Shareable Quotes from Experts about the Impact of Digital Life," July 3, 2018. www.pewinternet.org/2018/07/03/shareable-quotes-from-experts-about-the-impact-of-digital-life.

Chapter Four:
Open to Everyone

22. Quoted in Mayo and Newcomb, "How the Web Was Won."

23. Tom McKay, "Amazon's First Automated Brick-and-Mortar Store Opens to the Public on Monday," Gizmodo. January 21, 2018. gizmodo.com/ amazons-first-automated-brick-and-mortar-store-opens-to-1822277611.

24. J. R. Okin, *The Information Revolution*. Winter Harbor, ME: Ironbound, 2005, p. 222.

25. Quoted in BBC News, "Scandalous Scoop Breaks Online," January 30, 1998. news.bbc.co.uk/1/hi/events/clinton_under_fire/the_big_picture/50031. stm.

26. Gregg Russell, "Pandora's Web?," CNN Interactive, January 30, 1998. www.cnn.com/ALLPOLITICS/1998/01/30/pandora.web.

27. Quoted in Russell, "Pandora's Web?"

28. Quoted in Mayo and Newcomb, "How the Web Was Won."

29. Quoted in Mayo and Newcomb, "How the Web Was Won."

30. Daniel Akst, "Take Me Out to the Internet? Tune In to Baseball on the Web," *Los Angeles Times*, September 6, 1995, p. D1.

Epilogue:
A New Era of Instant Information

31. Quoted in Mayo and Newcomb, "How the Web Was Won."

32. Quoted in Mayo and Newcomb, "How the Web Was Won."

33. Quoted in Roberto V. Zicari, "Interview with Jimmy Wales," ODMBS, February 21, 2009. www.odbms.org/blog/2009/02/interview-with-jimmy-wales.html.

34. Olivia Solon and Emma Graham-Harrison, "The Six Weeks that Brought Cambridge Analytica Down," *The Guardian*, May 3, 2018. www.theguardian.com/uk-news/2018/may/03/cambridge-analytica-closing-what-happened-trump-brexit.

35. Steven Rosenbaum, "Why the Fake News Debate Gets It Wrong," *Forbes*, December 12, 2016. www.forbes.com/sites/stevenrosenbaum/2016/12/12/why-the-fake-news-debate-gets-it-wrong/#3ca0f9051764.

For More Information

Books

Blumenthal, Karen. *Steve Jobs: The Man Who Thought Different*. New York, NY: Square Fish, 2012.
> Blumenthal provides a look at the man who created Apple computers, from his college days to his inventions to his death from cancer.

Csiszar, John. *Information Technology (STEM in Current Events)*. Broomall, PA: Mason Crest, 2016.
> This book introduces information technology, describing the development of the internet, smartphones, data storage systems, and cloud computing.

Harris, Ashley Rae. *Microsoft: The Company and its Founders*. Edina, MN: Essential Library, 2012.
> Harris presents a company profile of Microsoft and its famous founder, Bill Gates.

Kallen, Stuart. *Jeff Bezos and Amazon*. San Diego, CA: Reference Point Press, 2016.
> Learn about Jeff Bezos's upbringing and how he founded of the biggest online company in the world.

Kassnoff, David. *What Degree Do I Need to Pursue a Career in Information Technology and Information Systems?* New York, NY: Rosen Young Adult, 2016.
> Find out what it takes to develop a career in information technology and information systems.

Meyer, Terry Teague. *The Vo-Tech Track to Success in Information Technology*. New York, NY: Rosen Classroom, 2015.
> This guide to how young people can pursue a career in information technology includes tips, resources, and real-world examples from people in the field.

Redding, Anna Crowley. *Google It: A History of Google*. New York, NY: Feiwel and Friends, 2018.
> This books tells the story of two Stanford University students who set out to organize the world's information.

Websites

Fiveminded

fiveminded.com/history-of-the-internet-animated-for-kids

This website has a video and text about the history of the internet.

Gizmodo

gizmodo.com

One of the largest tech blogs on the internet, this website highlights technology "you never knew you always wanted."

Mashable

mashable.com

A current stream of news in technology, social media trends, and entertainment is offered here.

National Geographic Kids: Fake News

kids.nationalgeographic.com/explore/ngk-sneak-peek/april-2017/fake-news/

This website has an excellent article on understanding and spotting fake news.

New York Public Library: Internet Safety Tips

nypl.org/help/about-nypl/legal-notices/internet-safety-tips

This is a helpful source of information about internet safety for teens.

Pew Research Center

pewinternet.org

This website is known worldwide for its surveys and statistics. In its section on internet and technology, there are articles, statistics, and more that illustrate the impact of the information revolution.

Index

local area network (LAN), 59

M

Markoff, John, 35
Massachusetts Institute of Technology (MIT), 29–30, 49, 51, 58
Mauchly, John W., 16, 18–21, 23
McCarthy, John, 35
Medium-Scale Integration (MSI) chips, 31
Metcalf, Robert, 59
microchips, 10, 27, 31
microprocessors, 34, 44, 69
Microsoft, 6, 45, 64, 71, 76, 80
modems, 36, 48–49, 74, 77–78, 80
mouse, 36–37, 40, 71, 80
MoveOn.org, 76

N

National Aeronautics and Space Administration (NASA), 27, 29, 36, 83
net neutrality, 7, 90–91
Noyce, Robert, 26–27
number systems, 13, 16

O

Okin, J. R., 69
On-Line Man-Computer Communication (Licklider), 51
oNLine System (NLS), 36–38

P

Page, Larry, 7

personal computer (PC), 7, 31, 40, 45–46
printers, 29, 59
privacy, 88–89
protocols, 60–63
punch cards, 27, 29, 36

R

Roberts, Larry, 53
Rometty, Ginni, 58
Rosenbaum, Steven, 92
routers, 55, 59, 60
Royko, Mike, 65
Russell, Gregg, 74
Russell, Stephen, 35

S

search engines, 64, 68–71
    See also Google
Semi-Automatic Ground Environment (SAGE), 49
Shockley, William B., 25
smartphones, 8, 13, 68, 83, 92
Smiley, Jane, 16
social networks, 83, 85
    See also Facebook
Soviet Union, 20–21, 49–50
Sputnik, 49–50
Stanford University, 34–36, 55, 69
streaming, 76–78, 81

T

Taylor, Robert, 51, 53
Telenet, 48
Texas Instruments, 25, 27, 31, 34

Picture Credits

Cover Zapp2Photo/Shutterstock.com; pp. 6–7 (background) Oleksandr Rupeta/ NurPhoto via Getty Images; pp. 6 (left), 10–11, 17, 19 Bettmann/Bettmann/Getty Images; p. 6 (right) © Doug Wilson/Corbis/Corbis via Getty Images; p. 7 (top) Juana Arias/The Washington Post/Getty Images; p. 7 (bottom left) Kim Kulish/ Corbis via Getty Images; p. 7 (bottom right) Chip Somodevilla/Getty Images; p. 9 ullstein bild/ullstein bild via Getty Images; pp. 14–15, 22–23 Underwood Archives/Getty Images; p. 24 Keystone-France/Gamma-Keystone via Getty Images; p. 26 Yoshikazu Tsuno/Gamma-Rapho via Getty Images; pp. 28–29 Bert Hardy Advertising Archive/Getty Images; p. 32 Indianapolis Museum of Art/ Getty Images; p. 33 Yoshikazu Tsuno/AFP/Getty Images; pp. 37, 60–61 Apic/ Getty Images; pp. 38–39 Harold M. Lambert/Lambert/Getty Images; p. 42 SSPL/Getty Images; p. 44 Mark Madeo/Future Publishing via Getty Images; p. 50 Sovfoto/UIG via Getty Images; pp. 52–53 Philip Preston/The Boston Globe via Getty Images; p. 54 Jay L. Clendenin/Los Angeles Times via Getty Images; pp. 56–57 Bob Rowan/Corbis via Getty Images; p. 64 Alexander Hassenstein/ Getty Images; p. 67 Paul Souders/Getty Images; pp. 70–71 Evan Lorne/ Shutterstock.com; pp. 72–73 John G. Mabanglo/AFP/Getty Images; p. 75 Getty Images/Hulton Archive/Getty Images; p. 77 Pe3k/ Shutterstock.com; p. 81 Linda Bestwick/Shutterstock.com; p. 82 Nicholas Kamm/AFP/Getty Images; p. 84 Andrei Minsk/Shutterstock.com; p. 85 Benny Marty/Shutterstock.com; pp. 86–87 Roman Pyshchyk/Shutterstock.com; p. 89 Michael Candelori/Shutterstock.com; p. 90 Wiktor Szymanowicz/Barcroft Media via Getty Images.

About the Author

Tamra B. Orr is the author of more than 500 nonfiction/educational books for readers of all ages. She graduated from Ball State University in Muncie, Indiana, with a degree in English and Education. She planned on becoming an English teacher. Instead, she moved to Oregon and began writing books. She remembers kicking and screaming on the way to getting her first computer, sure she would never learn how to use it. Today, she is on her ninth computer and while she knows how to use it very well, she has no idea how it actually works.